MYSTERIES IN AMERICAN ARCHEOLOGY

Walker's American History
series for young people

NON-FICTION

Incredible Constructions and the People Who Built Them
Mel Boring
Mississippi Steamboatman: The Story of Henry Miller Shreve
Edith McCall
Mysteries in American Archeology
Elsa Marston
Who Put the Cannon in the Courthouse Square:
A Guide to Uncovering the Past
Kay Cooper

FICTION

Away to Fundy Bay (Nova Scotia, 1775)
Katherine McGlade Marko
Message from the Mountains (Missouri, 1826)
Edith McCall
Straight Along a Crooked Road (crossing America, 1850)
Marilyn Cram Donahue
The Stratford Devil (Connecticut, 1651)
Claude Clayton Smith
What About Annie? (Maryland, the Great Depression)
Claudia Mills
Which Way Freedom? (South Carolina, 1861–1864)
Joyce Hansen

Mysteries in American Archeology

Elsa Marston

Walker and Company
New York

Walker's American History Series for Young People
Frances Nankin, Series Editor

First published in the United States of America in 1986 by the Walker Publishing Company, Inc.

Published simultaneously in Canada by John Wiley & Sons Canada, Limited, Rexdale, Ontario.

Library of Congress Cataloging-in-Publication Data

Marston, Elsa.
Mysteries in American archeology.
(Walker's American history series for young people)
Includes index.
1. United States—Antiquities—Juvenile literature.
2. Indians of North America—Antiquities—Juvenile literature. 3. Archaeology—United States—History—Juvenile literature. 4. Excavations (Archaeology)—United States—Juvenile literature. I. Title.
II. Series.
E159.5.M29 1986 973.1 85-20259
ISBN 0-8027-6608-0
ISBN 0-8027-6627-7 (reinforced)

Book design by Teresa M. Carboni

Printed in the United States of America

10 9 8 7 6 5 4 3 2 1

For my mother, Harriet Marston . . .
always eager to know about the world

CONTENTS

ACKNOWLEDGMENTS

For their valuable contributions in offering information and interpretation, and in reviewing chapters, the author wishes to thank the following persons: James Gilmore, writer, Santa Barbara, California; David Hazzard, archeologist, Research Center for Archeology, Yorktown, Virginia; Robert Heyder, superintendent, and the archeological staff, Mesa Verde National Park, Mesa Verde, Colorado; Richard Humphrey, writer and archeologist, Kingston, Massachusetts; William Iseminger, archeologist and site interpreter, Cahokia Mounds Historic Site, East St. Louis, Illinois; Dr. James Kellar, professor of archeology, Indiana University, Bloomington, Indiana; Daniel Leary, avocational archeologist, Pembroke, New Hampshire; Dr. Patrick Munson, professor of anthropology, Indiana University; Peter Nebergall, graduate student in archeology, Indiana University; Dr. Ann Otteson, archeologist, Resource Analysts, Bloomington, Indiana; Dr. Dennis Stanford, curator, Department of Anthropology, National Museum of Natural History, Smithsonian Institution, Washington, D.C.; Birgitta Wallace, archeologist, Parks Canada—Archeology, Halifax, Nova Scotia; and Dr. Ray Williamson, project director, U.S. Congress Office of Technology Assessment, Washington, D.C.

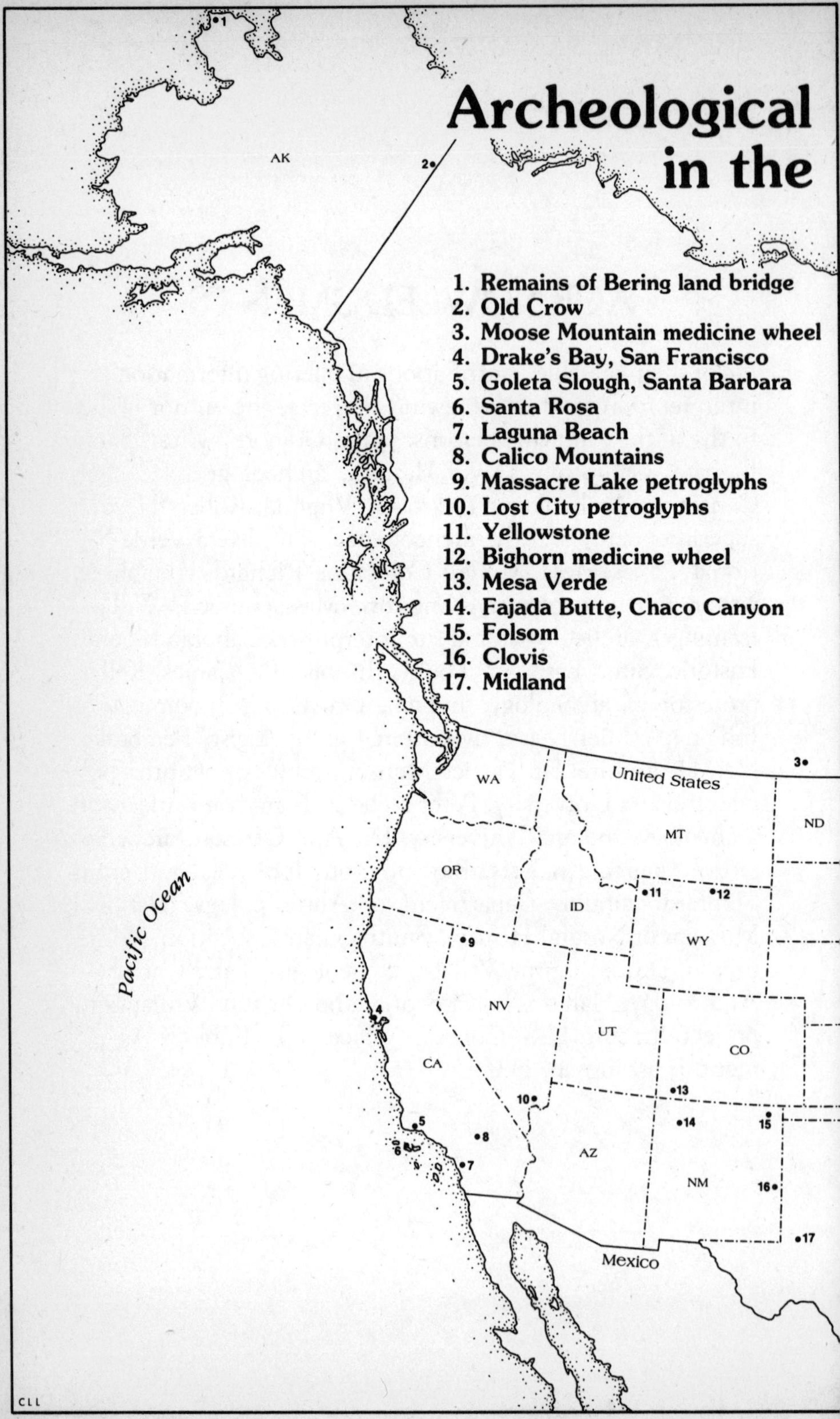
Archeological
in the
1. Remains of Bering land bridge
2. Old Crow
3. Moose Mountain medicine wheel
4. Drake's Bay, San Francisco
5. Goleta Slough, Santa Barbara
6. Santa Rosa
7. Laguna Beach
8. Calico Mountains
9. Massacre Lake petroglyphs
10. Lost City petroglyphs
11. Yellowstone
12. Bighorn medicine wheel
13. Mesa Verde
14. Fajada Butte, Chaco Canyon
15. Folsom
16. Clovis
17. Midland
AK
United States
WA
MT
ND
OR
ID
WY
NV
UT
CO
CA
AZ
NM
Mexico
Pacific Ocean
CLL

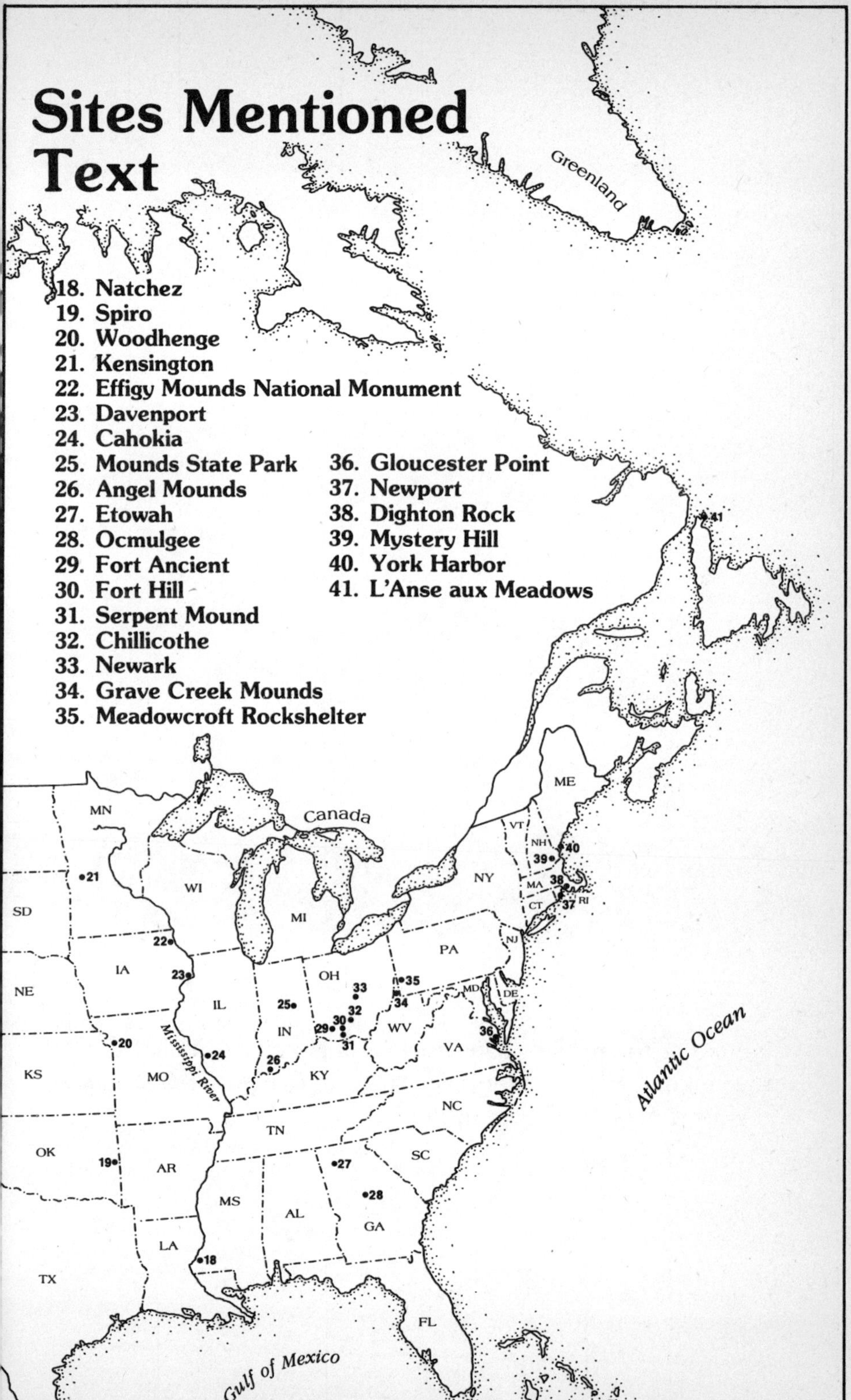
Sites Mentioned Text
18. Natchez
19. Spiro
20. Woodhenge
21. Kensington
22. Effigy Mounds National Monument
23. Davenport
24. Cahokia
25. Mounds State Park
26. Angel Mounds
27. Etowah
28. Ocmulgee
29. Fort Ancient
30. Fort Hill
31. Serpent Mound
32. Chillicothe
33. Newark
34. Grave Creek Mounds
35. Meadowcroft Rockshelter
36. Gloucester Point
37. Newport
38. Dighton Rock
39. Mystery Hill
40. York Harbor
41. L'Anse aux Meadows
Greenland
Canada
Atlantic Ocean
Gulf of Mexico
Mississippi River
MN
WI
MI
NY
ME
VT
NH
MA
CT
RI
SD
IA
NE
IL
IN
OH
PA
NJ
MD
DE
WV
VA
KY
MO
KS
OK
AR
TN
NC
SC
MS
AL
GA
LA
TX
FL

Note: For the reader's convenience, a glossary is included at the end of the book. Words appearing in the glossary are *italic* the first time they appear in the text.

1

What Can Archeology Tell About Mysteries of the Past?

THE world is full of mysteries left by people of the past. Some are well known, such as the huge Pyramids of Egypt, tombs of ancient kings; the mystic circles of massive stones at Stonehenge in England; and the lost city of the Incas, Macchu Picchu, high on a mountaintop in Peru. In this country, too, there are lost cities, pyramids, and stonehenges. What secrets do they hide? What clues do they hold that tell about the people who made them?

Some people of the past left behind written records, such as books, letters, shopping lists, or words carved on statues and buildings. We can learn about those people by studying their *history.* But if they left no written records, the only way we can know about them is through *archeology.* Archeology is the study of people who lived in the past by finding and examining whatever they left behind—other than written things.

Archeologists used to be interested mainly in the fine buildings and the beautiful or unusual objects created by early civilizations. Today, however, they want to know as much as possible about the people. They try to learn about the poor workers as well as the rulers, the huts and caves as well as the temples. The supper of a poor farmer may be as important to an archeologist as a queen's earrings. Archeologists hope to find out what people did every day, what their sicknesses were, how they got along with others—everything that can be learned about them.

The place an archeologist studies is called a *site.* Most clues about what people did in past centuries have become covered with soil, so archeologists usually have to dig, or *excavate,* to uncover them.

Anything archeologists find as they excavate a site may have some value. Carved figurines are important, but so are scraps of pottery and stone tools. These things are called *artifacts.* To an archeologist, the word artifact means any object that is made, or in some way used, by human beings. Seeds and animal bones are useful finds because they show what people ate. Even different-colored streaks of soil can be important because they may show where a fire once burned, or a wooden post or building once stood.

Archeologists have learned to put together the various clues they find to help explain how people lived in the past. They make intelligent guesses about some of the more puzzling questions. The task requires using very careful methods. Just as a detective must take good notes and not disturb evidence at the scene of a crime, archeologists have to work in a precise manner. They keep detailed records of everything they find and note the exact spot in which every artifact is discovered.

To be useful to an archeologist, artifacts have to be found where they were left by the people who made or used them. Usually they are found with other things left at about the same time. The place where an artifact is found at a site, along with the objects and soil around it, is called the *context.* A site that has been dug into carelessly, or robbed of some of the objects it once contained, can be a nightmare for archeologists. If artifacts are moved from their contexts, many important clues about the people who made them are lost.

Archeologists also must try to date the artifacts they find. If they know how old a thing is—a piece of wood or pottery, for example—they have a good idea about when the people who used it were living at the site. Scientists have developed several ways of *dating* objects and are continually trying to make these methods more accurate. One technique, called *radiocarbon dating,* is especially important. By measuring, in special laboratories, the amount of radioactive carbon left in the remains of a long-dead plant or animal, the approximate time in the past when it lived can be determined.

No dating technique, however, works for every type of artifact. Most, including radiocarbon dating, do not give very accurate dates. Sometimes an approximate date is all that is needed, but there is always the possibility that pieces of an archeological puzzle may not fit together because of an incorrect date.

Archeologists express dates in two ways. In recent years the term B.P., or "Before the Present," has come into use. It means about the same thing as "years ago." This is helpful for using long-ago dates, such as 12,000 B.P., which means "12,000 years ago." However, for more recent dates the B.C./A.D. system is often more convenient. In this book, both systems will be used where appropriate.

Learning about how people lived in the past helps us to better understand our own society. We can begin to understand a little more of the whole history of human beings, with all the wonderful and terrible and astonishing things they have done. And we can learn something about ourselves, for we, too, are a part of that history.

Few clues in archeology, however, are enough to unlock a mystery of the past. Archeologists rarely discover precise answers. They have to do the best they can with what they find. Still, their job is to try to find answers to some fascinating, baffling questions about people—and that makes archeology exciting.

This book is about some of those mysteries. Though mysterious now, they may be better understood tomorrow, thanks to the work of archeologists today and in the future.

2

When Did the First Americans Arrive?

LONG ago, thousands of years back in time, a small group of hunters broke up their simple camp and started on their way again. They were following herds of caribou and large elephants called mammoths, for they depended on these animals for food and clothing. The weather was cold and raw, the land bleak with little vegetation besides long grasses. These brown-skinned, black-haired people were hardy, however, and able to survive the harsh conditions. They had known no other kind of life, even in the northwest part of Asia where they had lived earlier.

This is how the first people came to the continent of North America, a land that had had no human beings up until that time. The people did not know they had reached a new land. The plains simply stretched before them, and they followed the wandering herds of animals.

They came during the *Ice Age,* a time of heavy glaciation that lasted until about 10,000 B.P. Immense layers of snow and ice covered North America as far south as Illinois. During long periods when more snow fell than could melt, the glacier would build up. The cold periods were followed by slightly warmer periods. The glacier would shrink, then build up again and spread, then shrink again. This happened many times, over hundreds of thousands of years.

Curiously enough, the Ice Age was what made it possible for people to cross from Siberia to Alaska. As the ice cap expanded, it drew great amounts of water from the sea, and this caused the sea level to drop. The water in the Bering Strait between Siberia and Alaska—a passageway only fifty-six miles wide today—is shallow. When the sea level dropped, land was exposed, making a wide bridge between Asia and North America. Scientists call this the Bering land bridge. Up to 1,300 miles wide, it was never covered by ice. The central part of Alaska was also free of ice. There was nothing to prevent the large herd animals in Siberia from crossing to the other continent, nor the hunters from following them.

The people may have started their long walk eastward around 40,000 B.P., or even earlier. As they slowly moved across central Alaska, they came to the ice-covered area. Yet here, too, scientists believe there was a passageway. Canada lay under two great sheets of ice. Between them, running approximately north and south, was a narrow stretch of bare land. This ice-free corridor, perhaps one hundred to five hundred miles wide, led down through western Canada to the Great Plains.

The passageway was not always open because, at times, the ice sheets grew larger and joined. Scientists have different views about when it was open and when closed, but they seem to agree that it was closed at least from 18,000 B.P. until sometime around 13,000 B.P. Aside from that period, the migrating people probably had an open—if cold and windy—path from Alaska to Montana.

Around 12,000 B.P., the last glacial advance began to retreat. As the ice cap melted, the water in the ocean rose again. By 10,000 or 9,000 B.P., the two continents were once more separated by water. Without the Bering land bridge, people could no longer walk to this continent from Asia. Nor could anyone go back. By that time, however, enough people had reached America. As their numbers increased, they were soon moving to all parts of the Western Hemisphere including down to the tip of South America. A new population was growing.

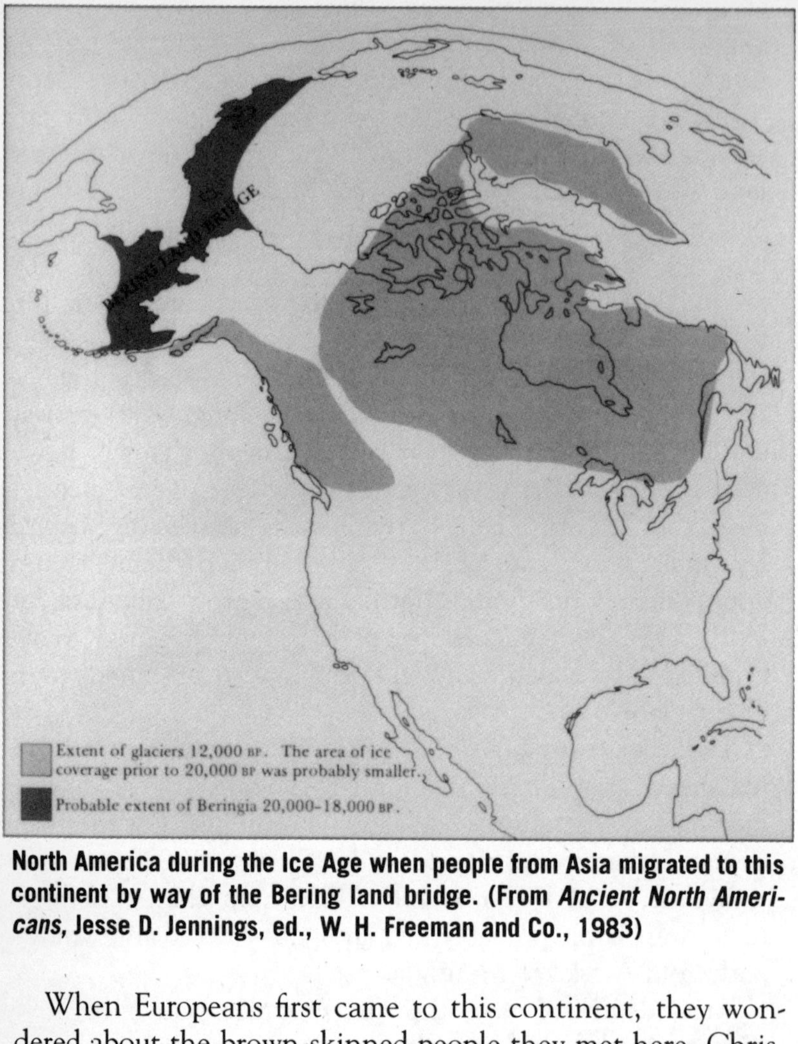

North America during the Ice Age when people from Asia migrated to this continent by way of the Bering land bridge. (From *Ancient North Americans,* Jesse D. Jennings, ed., W. H. Freeman and Co., 1983)

When Europeans first came to this continent, they wondered about the brown-skinned people they met here. Christopher Columbus called them Indians, thinking he had reached the Indies in Asia. Soon, however, it became evident that this was a different land. All sorts of ideas were suggested to explain who the inhabitants could be. Some people thought they were descended from Israelites who had wandered here from the Bible lands some fifteen hundred or two thousand years back. Others thought they might be descended from Vikings, or even an ancient people from Asia called Scythians.

In 1590, a Spanish priest wrote a book about the Indians. He hit fairly close to the truth when he said that the American peoples had come from Asia by an overland route. As Europeans learned more about the world and made better maps, this idea began to make sense. After all, the northwestern part of North America was very close to Siberia, and the American Indians looked much like peoples of Asia. In the nineteenth century, with more knowledge about geology and climate, most people came to accept the theory of the land link between Siberia and Alaska.

Though archeologists today agree that this is the way human beings first reached America, the question of when they came is far from settled. It is, in fact, one of the hottest ongoing questions in archeology, a mystery that arouses a lot of investigation and debate.

Early in this century, archeologists started to look seriously for traces of the first Americans. Paleo-Indians was the name they gave these people, *paleo* meaning ancient. Not much headway was made at first, however. At that time an important scholar named Aleš Hrdlička insisted that human beings could not have been here for more than a few thousand years. At first he only wanted to put an end to unscientific claims and false ideas about the Paleo-Indians that had been popular in the nineteenth century. His views became so fixed, however, that he discouraged other archeologists in their research. Even as late as the 1920s many people believed that the Indians had come only two or three thousand years ago—in spite of what was known about the Bering land bridge.

The breakthrough came in 1926—thanks to a cowboy. One spring day, the cowhand was riding through the countryside near the small town of Folsom, New Mexico, looking for a lost cow. He noticed a large, unusual bone sticking out of the soil by a dried-up streambed. Curious, he got out his knife and scraped away some dirt, which revealed more bones. Nearby was a spear tip of carefully chipped stone, about two inches long. Neither the spear tip nor the bones looked like any the cowboy had ever seen. He took samples home and told his friends about his find. Before long, some of these strange bones were sent to J. D. Figgins, director of the Colorado Museum of Natural History.

What Figgins and his team of archeologists soon found at Folsom were the bones of a large kind of superbison. They knew it had become extinct many thousands of years ago. Close to the bones they discovered another broken spear point. But the fact that the point was near the bones was not enough proof that it had actually killed the animal. For various reasons, objects from different periods in the past can sometimes end up near each other.

Figgins continued to work at the Folsom site, and in 1927 he found the proof he needed. In the skeleton of another superbison was a spear tip stuck between two of the animal's ribs. It could only have been put there by the force of a man's arm. Here was clear evidence. People were on the American continent when that kind of bison was still alive—more than ten thousand years ago!

This exciting discovery encouraged archeologists. They started looking for evidence that would give a more accurate idea of the time when people first came to America. More spear tips, which are usually called *projectile points,* were soon found in other places in the Southwest. They were like the ones discovered at Folsom. Archeologists now believe the Folsom points were made between 11,000 and 10,500 B.P

Then came another giant step forward in the search. In 1932, a different type of stone projectile point turned up. This was called the Clovis point because it was first found near Clovis, New Mexico. Though discovered later, Clovis points date from an earlier time, around 12,000 to 11,000 B.P. The two kinds of points are found with different kinds of animal bones: the Clovis points with mammoth bones, and the Folsom points with bison and smaller animals.

Both types of points, on the other hand, are crafted with great skill and are easy to identify. The Clovis points are the longer of the two, up to five inches in length. Other well-

A band of early Americans, probably using Folsom points, about to kill some large bison cornered in a canyon, around 10,500 B.P. A diorama. (Mesa Verde Museum, National Park Service)

made stone and bone tools are sometimes discovered with Clovis points. This *tool kit* suggests that these early people developed a good technology for their needs.

The Clovis points, however, raise a very puzzling question. They are numerous and have been found over most of this country, from Arizona to Nova Scotia. It is as if the early Americans who used these points appeared almost everywhere within a few hundred years after 12,000 B.P. But did they already have the Clovis point when they reached the Great Plains, or did they develop it after they arrived? No clues have yet been found in the places where they might have started making the point before reaching the Great Plains. This is partly because conditions for excavation in Alaska and Northwest Asia are difficult, and because any early sites in the ice-free passage were probably destroyed by the last advance of the glacier.

Early man projectile points; replicas of points made by Paleo-Indians. Folsom points are in the person's left hand and at the top of the picture; the larger point on the left is a Clovis point. (Arizona State Museum, University of Arizona; photographer, E. B. Sayles)

At any rate, the early Americans found the open grassland of the Great Plains a familiar type of environment, with the same kinds of large animals they already knew. Apparently they felt at home. With plenty of room, plenty of food, and little disease, the people seem to have increased their numbers rapidly. The population may have grown so fast, in fact, that the hunters killed off too many of the mammoths that were their favorite prey. This is probably why the Folsom points are not found with mammoth bones. As the mammoths grew scarce in one area, the people would move on. In this way, Paleo-Indians could have covered most of the continent in five hundred to a thousand years, taking their Clovis points and tool kits with them.

This "population explosion"—if that is what happened—suggests to some archeologists that human beings were not present in this land before approximately 12,000 B.P. Otherwise, because conditions such as climate and availability of food were much the same earlier, the people would have increased and spread far and wide at an earlier time. They would have left plenty of projectile points and bone tools as evidence. So far, however, such evidence has not been found.

Nevertheless, many other archeologists believe that the first Americans arrived long before 12,000 B.P. In the last twenty years or so, discoveries have been made that seem to indicate earlier dates for the first-comers. None of these dates, however, are accepted yet by all archeologists as accurate.

For example, a place called Meadowcroft Rockshelter in western Pennsylvania was excavated in the mid-1970s. Archeologists from the University of Pittsburgh found many layers of soil with traces of fire pits from different times. They claim that some bits of charcoal and a scrap of basket, dated by the radiocarbon technique, appear to be more than nineteen thousand years old. But other archeologists say that these dates are not possible, in light of what is known about the climate and plant and animal life at that time.

Another early site is Old Crow in east-central Alaska, which was excavated in the 1960s and 1970s. It has been called the oldest site yet found. From a bed of fossils revealed by river erosion, archeologists found bones that look as though human beings had worked on them. There were mammoth bones that had been crushed to expose the marrow, and a tool made from a caribou bone. These artifacts have been dated by the radiocarbon technique to a period between 30,000 and 24,000 B.P. But questions remain. The bone tool was not found in the place where it was originally put down; it had apparently been carried by a stream sometime in the past. And, as always, the radiocarbon dates are not one hundred percent reliable.

Other researchers have examined sites that suggest even earlier dates. One puzzling place is an island called Santa Rosa thirty miles off the coast of Southern California. It could have been reached easily during the Ice Age when the water was lower. In 1976, archeologists found a fire pit exposed in a gully. In it were some bones of dwarf mammoths, along with stone tools. Bits of charcoal from the fire area appeared to be older than forty thousand years. Were Paleo-Indians having elephant barbecues on Santa Rosa Island more than forty thousand years ago? Some archeologists think so. Others disagree, however, saying that the fire must have resulted from natural causes and the stone tools were made much later.

Louis S. B. Leakey, the famous archeologist who worked in Africa and found traces there of the earliest known humans, also looked into the question of the first Americans. In 1963, at Calico Mountains in California, he examined a site where stones that looked like simple tools had been found at an excavated depth of twenty-four feet. Other stones nearby appeared to be arranged like a fire hearth. Scientists agree that the soil layers are at least forty to seventy thousand years old. Dr. Leakey believed that the Calico site could have been used by man as long ago as that.

But was it a human being who chipped those "tools" and arranged that stone "hearth"—or was it nature? Other scientists who have examined the site believe the stones are geofacts, broken and left in place by nature, and not artifacts. There is still no certain evidence of seventy-thousand-year-old Americans.

Archeologists have found many artifacts that indicate the presence of early Americans—but what about evidence of the people themselves? Very ancient human bones have been much harder to find. Animal bones are plentiful, but bones of people from ancient times almost never turn up. When they do, estimating how old they are is a very difficult task and causes much disagreement.

In 1933, a boy named Howard Wilson, who liked to hunt for Indian relics, came upon a nearly-buried bone near his home in Laguna Beach, California. Thinking it might be human, he dug it out. It turned out to be part of a human skull. Wilson took it home and kept it, in spite of his mother's advice to throw it out. Two years later he sent a careful drawing of the skull to a museum, asking what the experts there could tell him about it. They replied that the skull was prehistoric, but not extremely old.

Wilson still believed his find was different from other ancient skulls he had seen in museums. Due to his persistence, over the next twenty-two years the skull was sent to laboratories and museums in both the United States and Europe. It was even sent to Africa, where Dr. Leakey examined it in 1967. Scientists' opinions about its age varied greatly. Finally the skull was analyzed by the radiocarbon method. The results suggested that it was somewhere between 15,700 and 18,600 years old. That would make the Laguna Beach skull the oldest human remains yet found in this country. Many archeologists, however, do not accept this view because the radiocarbon dates may be wrong and because the skull was not excavated and recorded in the proper way.

A skull that is widely believed to be the oldest yet found was discovered in 1953 in Midland, Texas, in a blow-out. A blow-out is a spot where the soil has blown away, leaving anything somewhat heavy behind. At such a site, archeologists may have to deal with a situation in which ancient bones or tools rest beside Coke bottles. In spite of the difficulties presented by these conditions, a large team of archeologists, geologists, and other scientists carefully studied the Midland skull and the place where it was found. Finally they agreed that the owner of the skull had lived more than ten thousand years ago, possibly as much as twenty thousand!

The search goes on for remains of a much earlier human being. Sometimes newer methods of dating are used. By means of a recently developed technique, a group of researchers have dated some human bones found in California at forty to fifty thousand years old. However, the technique they used is still not well understood and presents many problems.

Mammoth hunt diorama shows Paleo-Indians using what were probably Clovis points to attack a mammoth, sometime around 11,500 B.P. (Arizona State Museum, University of Arizona; photographer, Helga Teiwes)

Other scientists, using an advanced and much more reliable form of radiocarbon dating, report that their tests of these bones indicate ages no older than eleven thousand years.

Today, archeologists can say with certainty only that people have been here for twelve thousand years. Though it is possible that the first Americans arrived thousands of years earlier, there is still no clear proof. The Clovis points dating from around 12,000 B.P. are the only proof that everyone accepts. Perhaps tomorrow archeologists will find something that changes the picture. Then we may have a more accurate answer to the question that has puzzled people for so long: When *did* the first Americans arrive?

3

Who Really Discovered America?

PEOPLE from Asia reached this country at least twelve thousand years ago, but Europeans were latecomers. So far as anyone knows, Christopher Columbus was the first to arrive and to leave proof of it. For many years, however, people have wondered whether Columbus and his men really were the first to come from the Old World. Couldn't visitors from across the Atlantic have reached this continent many centuries earlier?

Some people insist that this, in fact, did happen. It is said, for example, that Vikings settled in New England and explored as far inland as Minnesota and Oklahoma. Mysterious mounds in Ohio have been described as forges where Celts, an ancient people of Western Europe, made iron into tools and weapons. Egyptians and Greeks are said to have mined copper in Michigan, and Phoenicians, some say, came from the eastern Mediterranean to trade with Native Americans thousands of years ago.

It is exciting to suppose that visitors from the Old World—Europeans, Africans, people of the Middle East—were actually coming to America over a period of many years. The writers and groups who promote these ideas always find an eager audience. What proofs do they offer?

Carvings on rock are the kind of evidence most often described as proof of Old World visitors. Called *petroglyphs*, rock carvings have been found in this country from New England to California, and especially in the Southwest. Some

Petroglyphs found in north-central Arizona showing Indian clan symbols. ("MABURK" is probably the name of a more recent visitor to the site.) These are the sort of rock carvings sometimes said to have been made by ancient visitors from the Old World. (Rock Art Archives, University of California at Los Angeles; photographer, Helen Michaelis)

people say that many petroglyphs are really signs and symbols left by ancient travelers from the Old World.

Petroglyphs in Colorado, for example, supposedly look like symbols for the goddess of Carthage. Carthage was an empire on the coast of North Africa that existed twenty-five hundred years ago. Scratches on a rock at Massacre Lake in northwestern Nevada appear to be a Carthaginian prayer for rain. The ancient Carthaginians were well known as seamen, explorers, and traders. Some people believe they crossed the Atlantic to do business with the inhabitants of this continent—and apparently covered a lot of territory, if they reached Nevada.

The ancient Greeks, too, were traders and sailors. It is said that they also came to North America. A petroglyph in New Mexico is described as a Greek labyrinth design. Another rock carving found in Oklahoma appears to contain Greek letters and a crude sketch of a bull that looks like a constellation. Possibly, some say, Roman visitors also left messages, such as a Latin quotation carved on a rock near York Harbor, Maine.

Celts from both Spain and Ireland supposedly wrote messages on rock from one end of our country to the other. A petroglyph at a place called Lost City in southeastern Nevada has been explained as a description of the wool industry carried on by Celts in that area. Arabic letters carved on rock appear to show that Arabs made their way along the Atlantic seaboard and even to the western states. Marks found in mysterious stone chambers in Connecticut look like Christian symbols, suggesting that some Old World visitors may have been refugees from persecution in ancient times. And, it is claimed, many other peoples—Libyans, Berbers, Byzantine Greeks, Zoroastrians, Cypriots—all came to this land long ago and left their messages on rock.

Other bits of evidence are also described as proof of Old World visitors. Coins—Roman, Greek, Carthaginian, Byzantine—have turned up here and there, especially in the Eastern states. Hebrew coins found in Kentucky are said to have been left by Jewish refugees who fled to this continent after a rebellion against Roman rule in the second century A.D. A few unusual clay jars, similar to Roman jars found in the sea near Portugal, have been discovered just off the Maine coast. The writing of the Micmac Indians of Nova Scotia is said to have signs like ancient Egyptian hieroglyphics. In the Eastern states, boulders balanced on smaller rocks look like stone arrangements made by ancient Celts in Britain and Western Europe. Stone heads, described as Celtic or Carthaginian, have been dug up from Massachusetts soil.

Many more examples are offered by the people who make these claims. Anyone who would like to read more can turn to such books as *Saga America* and *Bronze Age America* by Barry Fell, *Lost America* by Arlington Mallery, *The Search for Lost America* by Salvatore Trento, and *Riddles in History* by Cyrus Gordon.

If Old World peoples really did visit this continent in ancient times, then surely archeological excavation should reveal some proof. After all, it is the job of archeologists to learn about the past by studying the things that people left behind. What, then, do American archeologists say about the rock carvings, coins, and buried objects?

Petroglyphs in this country have been carefully studied by professional archeologists and other scholars. These people are convinced that they were made by Native Americans. Many of the signs are messages easily understood as Indian sign language. In some cases, too, rocks have been marked in curious ways by glacial ice or by weathering. If certain marks look like writing found in the Old World, archeologists say, that is nothing but coincidence.

It is easy for imaginative persons to think up ways to explain rock carvings. People often see what they want to see, and believe what they want to believe. A large boulder called Dighton Rock, in the Taunton River in Massachusetts, is an excellent example of this. The figures carved on it were first examined in 1680 by an Englishman, who decided they were done by local Indians. A hundred years later, a Frenchman saw drawings of the figures and declared them Carthaginian. In the nineteenth century, a Danish scholar said they were a Viking message. Today, Portuguese scholars claim that the marks were made by sixteenth-century Portuguese explorers!

Petroglyphs are not too hard to fake, and some people have done this to get publicity and money, or to try to fool the scientists and the public. Genuine North American rock carvings are usually crude and often eroded. Therefore, a forger doesn't have to work very hard to make something that looks like the real thing. Buried, or exposed to harsh weather for a few years, the "ancient" rock carving will "age" very nicely.

The Kensington Stone, dug up in 1898 on a Minnesota farm, is probably the most famous example of a forged rock carving. This stone had a message inscribed on it in runes, a kind of writing used in the past in Scandinavian countries. For many years, some people believed that the stone really had been left by Vikings who reached the spot in 1362. But examination by scholars proved that the runes were written in a style much more modern than that used in fourteenth-century Sweden. The stone was, in fact, a hoax, possibly carved by the Swedish farmer who claimed to have discovered it on his land.

As for objects such as coins, stone heads, and vases, they prove little or nothing unless found in context. If the objects were laid down in the distant past, the soil would have built up over them in layers. By removing the layers systematically, archeologists can tell whether objects were left there long ago, or were deliberately buried in recent times. Also, artifacts usually are found together with other things from the same time period. A coin or figurine discovered all by itself looks suspiciously "planted."

Those who write popular books about ancient Old World visitors to America seem to give little importance to archeological excavation. They rarely mention careful examination of the usual traces that people of the past have left behind, such as ordinary tools and sites where the people lived. Nor do they say much about scientific dating of artifacts and sites. Their main interest is in remarkable discoveries, such as strange messages and objects that turn up in surprising places. This approach is very different from the archeologist's efforts to learn, through careful methods, about people of the past.

There is no reason to think that people could not have come to this continent from across the Atlantic long before Columbus. Many kinds of ancient boats were capable of making the trip. What archeologists and other scholars are saying is that no proof has been found that these ancient peoples did come. Perhaps someday a site in North America will come to light that everyone can agree is definitely Greek, or Carthaginian, or Celtic, or whatever. As yet, no such site has been discovered.

There is, however, one group of possible Old World visitors who do deserve serious attention. These are the Vikings. For a long time, people have thought that the Vikings, also called Norsemen, were certainly the first Europeans to visit our shores. It is said that early European explorers on the East Coast noticed some Indians who were unusually tall and light-skinned. A round stone tower in Newport, Rhode Island, still arouses much curiosity. Archeologists and historians say it was built as a watch tower by English settlers in the seventeenth century—but some people believe it was made by Norsemen hundreds of years earlier.

Other evidence suggesting that Vikings may have come to America can be found in the Norse sagas. These are stories written about seven or eight hundred years ago, at least two hundred years after the events they describe. They tell how Eric the Red, banished from Norway for his wild ways, settled in Iceland. Then he sailed west and started a colony on Greenland. Although it was anything but green, he called it Greenland to attract more settlers.

His son Leif Ericson, hearing of land still farther west, decided to search for it. This is supposed to have happened in the year A.D. 1000. According to the sagas, Leif sailed west and found a barren land that he named "Flat Stone Land," which is today's Baffin Island, near Greenland. Turning south, Leif came to a wooded shore that he called "Forest Land," today's Labrador. At last he reached a more inviting place with grassy meadows, a stream filled with salmon, and plenty of game. He called this place Vinland, the sagas tell us, because of a pleasant discovery made by one of his men. The fellow went exploring on his own and came back very excited. He had found, he reported, some vines with wild grapes, which would make wonderful wine.

This story has always been a puzzle. Although wild grapes can be found in New Brunswick, the part of Canada north of Maine, people used to think they grew only as far north as Massachusetts. If Leif and his men really did find grapes, it was argued, then Vinland must have been a relatively warm

The stone tower in Newport, Rhode Island, believed by some people to be Viking but which is in fact a seventeenth-century watch tower. (Newport Historical Society; photographer, John Hopf)

place, much farther south than Labrador and Newfoundland. Could Leif have sailed so far south before finding a good place to settle? Or, by naming the new land after the grapevines, was he, like his father, merely trying to make it sound better than it really was?

At any rate, for centuries people have been trying to find Ericson's Vinland. A number of spots on the East Coast, from Chesapeake Bay to Nova Scotia, appear to fit the descriptions in the sagas. One popular tradition says the Vikings settled on the Massachusetts coast near Plymouth. Another place is a Cape Cod pond where a researcher found what he believed were traces of a shelter for a Viking long boat. Newport, Rhode Island, seems a likely spot to some people because of the unusual stone tower mentioned earlier. But none of these places has provided archeological proof of the visits of Norsemen.

In 1960, a Norwegian archeologist named Helge Ingstad set out to explore the Atlantic coast from Rhode Island northward. He had a hunch where he might find something, but along the way he investigated all the sites that had been described as Norse.

In midsummer he reached the place he thought the most likely possibility. This was the northernmost tip of Newfoundland, a large island that is part of northeastern Canada. There, at a tiny, isolated fishing village called L'Anse aux Meadows, he asked the people if they knew of any traces of a long-ago settlement. The villagers took him to a nearby spot they called Indian Camp. Low grassy humps rose from the flat land. To Ingstad, they resembled traces of Norse sod houses, similar to those he had studied in Greenland and Iceland.

The next year, Ingstad started excavating with an archeological team. He soon found that the low humps and ridges were indeed remains of houses that looked like the old Norse ones. They had the same room layout, central fire pit, ember pits (to keep coals hot overnight), and earth benches along the walls. One structure, measuring about sixty-five by fifty-five feet, suggested a typical Viking long house. But the fact that these remains looked Norse did not prove that they were Norse—or that they were made as long ago as A.D. 1000.

In the third season of digging, the archeologists found a small stone spindle whorl, used for spinning wool. This was a significant find, since it was identical to known Viking spindle whorls. Spinning was the job of women, and therefore the artifact suggested something more. Women—and sheep to provide the wool—had apparently lived at the site. This implied that the settlers had hoped to stay there for some time.

One spindle whorl by itself, however, was still not enough proof. Little by little, other artifacts turned up—objects that were not the work of local Indians. One was a slender bronze pin like those used by Norsemen in the second half of the tenth century. Others were rusted nails, a simple oil lamp made from a round beach stone, and part of a bone needle.

Artifacts that helped prove the site at L'Anse aux Meadows was Viking: the stone lamp, hone for sharpening needles (lower left), spindle whorl (center), and piece of bone needle (right). (Parks Canada)

Then the archeologists found the remains of a crude smithy, where someone had worked with iron. The Norsemen, skillful blacksmiths, needed iron for boat nails and knew how to use a kind of iron found plentifully in the bogs nearby. The Indians never used iron, and there was no evidence of other Europeans at the site. This smithy was probably the first place anyone ever used iron in the New World!

By this time, the archeologists had three kinds of evidence: the ruins' similarity to known Viking structures; the kinds of artifacts, discovered in undisturbed soil; and radiocarbon dating of charcoal scraps. At last they knew the case for a Viking settlement was proven.

Questions remained, however. Why had the Norsemen decided to settle at L'Anse aux Meadows, and what did they do there? When excavation continued, this time by a Canadian team of archeologists, new discoveries came to light. Among them were a glass bead of a type used by tenth-century Norse people, and some objects preserved in waterlogged peat, which is a kind of soil made from decomposed plants. Besides many wood scraps from trimmed logs and planks, these objects included a sewn birchbark container and a piece of board from a boat.

The boat board and the large iron nails found earlier offered the best clues about what the Norse were doing at L'Anse aux Meadows. They apparently had used the settlement as a base camp for further explorations, returning to repair their boats at the site.

They probably went some distance down the St. Lawrence River. The Canadian archeologists found proof of these travels in the form of butternuts, discovered among the Norse objects. Butternuts, like wild grapes, grow in areas south of Newfoundland. If the Norse found butternuts, they may well have found grapes, too—though not very near L'Anse aux Meadows. This may explain the story of the happy explorer and the grapes: "Vinland" may have included the whole region of Newfoundland and New Brunswick.

Why, then, did the Vikings stay at L'Anse aux Meadows, when they knew of warmer places with more variety in food? A look at a map suggests the answer.

Home for these Norsemen was still Greenland, although it was a land with few natural resources. They used L'Anse aux Meadows as a halfway camp between that home and the southern parts of Vinland where they found the timber, furs, and other products—including wine—needed in Greenland. They could explore the New World in the summer, spend the winter comfortably at L'Anse aux Meadows, repair their boats, and sail back to Greenland when warm weather came again. Without the base in northern Newfoundland, they would have had to spend far too much time, especially in a short sailing season, voyaging the long distance back and forth. As it turned out, however, the Norse venture in Vinland did not last long, and the site at L'Anse aux Meadows appears to have been abandoned after only a few years.

Although archeologists agree that L'Anse aux Meadows could very well have been the settlement that Leif Ericson founded in Vinland, the proof that Leif himself lived there is still missing. Maybe it will never be found . . . or, possibly, another Viking site may come to light someday. In any case, we now know that the Norse sagas were based on truth. Vikings did reach the New World almost five hundred years before Columbus.

Helge Ingstad's discovery in Newfoundland is important for American archeology because thus far it is the only real evidence of Vikings on this continent. Moreover, the story shows how slowly and carefully archeologists often must work to find accurate information about people of long ago. At L'Anse aux Meadows no wonderful treasures or amazing messages came to light. Only humps of earth and little things such as pieces of wood and a glass bead were found. But through good guessing, hard work, and patience, these Norwegian and Canadian archeologists found an answer to a mystery that has fascinated people for hundreds of years.

4

Who Were the Mysterious Mound Builders?

AS pioneers moved west of the Appalachians soon after the American War of Independence, they met some surprising sights. The countryside was dotted with strange little hills—hundreds of thousands of them!

Some of these mounds were dramatic in appearance, rising like cones fifteen or twenty feet high. Many, however, were low and rounded. Others had steep sides and flat tops, like platforms. In parts of Ohio, ridges of earth called *earthworks* formed geometrical figures several hundred feet across. In still other places, long ridges crowned hilltops like fortifications. There were even mounds shaped like animals and birds!

Mounds had been seen in places before westward migration. In fact, Thomas Jefferson had excavated one in Virginia around 1781. It was not until the early nineteenth century, however, that people really began to wonder about these artificial hills. The mounds soon became a mystery that fascinated scholars and public alike.

To many people, the mounds suggested something exciting about the country that had not been suspected earlier. Though the new nation had great natural wealth, freedom, and good government, it lacked a long and glorious history. There were no fine monuments like those of Europe and Asia. The land appeared to be a wilderness where human beings had never achieved much in the past. But as more and more mounds were discovered, and some of their contents revealed,

A typical mound, Adena or Hopewell, in Indiana; pioneers saw many such mounds in the early nineteenth century. (Glen A. Black Laboratory of Archeology, Indiana University)

these heaps of earth began to arouse great interest. Could they have been left by some long-forgotten race with a high level of civilization? If so, then America might indeed have had a glorious past like that of the Old World.

People began talking about a vanished race of Mound Builders. Scholars, explorers, scientists, writers, and even poets offered their ideas about who the Mound Builders could have been. Today these ideas seem almost as interesting as what is actually known about the mounds and earthworks, and the people who built them.

Almost everyone agreed that the mysterious Mound Builders were not in any way connected with the American Indians. In those days, when white settlers were moving westward and trying to get the native people out of the way, the Indians were often criticized as savage, warlike tribes unskilled in crafts and agriculture. How, it was asked, could they have been capable of the planning and the steady labor needed to build the mounds? Most people believed the Mound Builders were as different from the Indians as day from night. Furthermore, the Indians with whom white people talked said they themselves did not know who had built the mounds. To many, that seemed definite proof that the native tribes and the Mound Builders were two entirely different peoples.

In contrast with the Indians' simple way of life, it was often pointed out, the Mound Builders seemed to have had a highly organized civilization. They had lived in settled communities, probably even cities, and they had practiced agriculture. In addition, many mounds contained beautiful things such as fine pottery and copper jewelry, so the vanished race appeared to have been very artistic, with a taste for luxury.

At first, nineteenth-century Americans assumed that all the mounds had been made at approximately the same time, by the same people. Mounds were to be seen from western New York to Iowa, from Minnesota to Florida. Therefore, it seemed as though the Mound Builders had had a unified state covering the whole central part of this country. And they must have been a large population! Since many of the mounds contained burials—some estimates were as high as a thousand burials per mound—then surely, people said, the countryside had once been heavily settled. According to another idea, certain large mounds covered the bodies of slain warriors. That made some people imagine huge and horrendous battles.

But when had this vanished race of highly-developed people lived? As scientists learned that the world was actually much older than had earlier been thought, it was claimed that the Mound Builders were one of the world's oldest civilizations. Whereas ancient mummies and skeletons in Egypt and Babylon were still well preserved, some writers pointed out, the bones in American mounds were usually crumbling "through age alone." (These writers must have ignored the differences in climate and soil; and, of course, almost nothing was known about dating ancient things at that time.)

Other attempts to figure out when the Mound Builders had lived only confused the picture. By counting the rings in large trees that had been growing on top of mounds, some people estimated that the artificial hills were only around five hundred years old. But the decay of the bones in the mounds suggested that the Mound Builders were far, far older. Then some mastodon bones were found in Missouri and Mississippi, with stone spear points among them. Around 1880, in mounds near Davenport, Iowa, two pipes turned up that were carved in an elephant-like shape. These discoveries made many people think that the Mound Builders had lived at the time of mammoths and mastodons. Maybe, it was said, they had even trained the great beasts to carry earth for the mounds!

Another discovery caused much debate. Articles made of beaten copper were found in many mounds. Did this prove, people wondered, that the Mound Builders knew how to work metals? Or had the persons buried in the mounds obtained the metal objects from Europeans? In that case, the mounds would be no more than two or three hundred years old.

If there were lots of different ideas about when the Mound Builders had lived, there were also as many about who they had been. Some people thought they must have come from Europe or what is now called the Middle East. One of the most popular ideas was that they were descended from the Tribes of Israel who had left Palestine about 2,600 B.P. Other people believed the mounds had been built by Vikings, or by Celts, Phoenicians, Egyptians, Romans, or Toltecs, a mysterious race said to have lived in Central America.

Imaginative writers suggested that Welshmen, under a legendary Prince Madoc, once colonized the land and built the mounds. Others said the Mound Builders might have come from Atlantis, a fabled island supposed to have disappeared under the sea thousands of years ago. When skeletons in Ohio mounds were measured and found to be fairly tall, about six feet, some people started talk about a race of giants. In short, the American public was willing to hear all sorts of stories about the wonderful Mound Builders.

Another question haunted the imaginations of nineteenth-century Americans. What had become of the Mound Builders? The only answer that seemed to make sense was that they were a peaceable people and had finally been overcome by warlike, barbaric invaders. William Henry Harrison, who later became president, was interested in the mounds. He expressed a typical view. After dreadful last-ditch battles in Ohio, he believed, the Mound Builders must have been forced to move on to Mexico where their descendents became the Aztecs.

For many years there was little challenge to these popular notions. In the second half of the nineteenth century, however, archeological methods and ideas were becoming more scientific, and a few individuals began to examine the mounds with greater care.

In the 1880s, John Wesley Powell, an explorer and expert on American Indians at the Smithsonian Institution, published a thorough study of Indian tribes. He had examined many mounds from Ohio to Mississippi and was convinced that the mounds had indeed been built by ancestors of present-day Indians. Furthermore, he said, there had never been just one race of Mound Builders. Instead, different Indian peoples had built different kinds of mounds at different times. Other scholars and the public gradually came to accept this view.

By the start of the twentieth century, accurate knowledge about the Indians who had built the mounds was beginning to replace the myths. Unfortunately, by that time a great many mounds and earthworks had been destroyed or severely damaged. This made it difficult for archeologists to study them in a systematic way.

There were several causes for the destruction. First, many pioneers had not understood or cared about the small hills in their fields, so they cut them away to make farming easier. Second, large numbers of mounds were clustered at places which were good locations for modern towns. They gave way to new cities such as Cincinnati and Chillicothe in Ohio; St. Louis, Missouri; and Chicago, Illinois. In addition, railroad lines demolished many earthworks. Mounds containing attractive artifacts, such as fine pottery that would fetch high prices from collectors, were looted by treasure-hunters.

In spite of this destruction, enough mounds remained for archeologists to study. Little by little, they put together information about the different mound-building peoples.

In 1901, archeologists excavated some mounds on the Adena estate located just outside Chillicothe, Ohio. They found that the mounds had been made in certain ways and contained certain types of objects. These particular characteristics of a *culture* are called *traits* in archeology. As other mounds with these same traits were discovered, archeologists decided that a distinct people had built them. They called these people and their culture Adena, using the name of the place where the mounds were first studied.

Although some earlier Indians had built small mounds, the Adena people were the first to build large ones. These people seem to have appeared in central Ohio, Kentucky, West Virginia, and parts of Indiana, possibly as early as 3000 B.P. They were apparently different from the Indians already living in the area, who had a simpler way of life that archeologists call *Archaic.* But where had the Adena people come from? The answer is not known. They may have migrated from lands east of Ohio, or possibly—because some Adena art looks like that of ancient Mexico—from Central America.

The trait that set the Adena people apart from other Indians of the region was their elaborate burial practices. They built the mounds to bury and honor their dead. The most respected persons, buried at the center of the mounds, were accompanied by many artifacts. These *grave gifts* included headdresses, masks, pieces of copper and mica, stone blades and tools, shell beads, and pottery.

Adena mounds were usually built in clusters. Some, however, were different. The largest is the Grave Creek Mound near Wheeling, West Virginia, which rises to a height of seventy feet. A famous earthwork, Serpent Mound, lies along a ridge above a stream in southwestern Ohio. It resembles a

Serpent Mound, one of the most spectacular Indian earthworks, lying on a ridge above a stream in Ohio. The serpent appears to be holding an egg in its jaws. (© 1982, Corson Hirschfeld)

twisting snake 1,254 feet long, and is believed to be Adena because objects from the Adena culture have been found in a burial mound nearby. The Serpent itself, however, gives no further clues. Who constructed this amazing and beautiful earthwork, and why? What could it mean? People have been wondering about Serpent Mound for more than one hundred and fifty years.

Gradually, archeologists believe, the Adena people gave way to a more powerful group of mound-building Indians known as Hopewell. As the Adena culture slowly declined, most of the people apparently moved out of their Ohio Valley homeland into Kentucky and farther south to the Tennessee Valley and Alabama. By about A.D. 400, the Adena ways had died out.

The Hopewell culture, discussed in the next chapter, appears to have lasted two or three hundred years longer. After its decline, mound-building ceased in the Ohio Valley and continued only in parts of the South. Then, sometime around A.D. 800 to 900, American Indians started building mounds again, and in an even more spectacular fashion. These new Mound Builders lived around the Mississippi River valley, with the Angel Mounds in Indiana the easternmost site. Their culture is therefore called Mississippian. They had permanent settlements, some almost like cities, and grew much of their food.

The mounds these Indians built were different from those of the Adena and Hopewell peoples. Only rarely containing burials, they were flat on top and served as sites for temples and other important buildings. Though the wooden structures that once stood on top of the mounds have long since disappeared, ramps of earth show that the mounds were meant to be climbed. Archeologists refer to this period of mound-building as the Temple Mound period.

In the South, the Mississippian culture took a somewhat different form. At places such as Etowah and Ocmulgee in Georgia and at Spiro, Oklahoma, the people made beautiful but very strange artifacts. Their art, as well as the shape of the mounds they constructed, is similar to that of ancient Mexico. Objects such as pottery, carved conch shells, and copper plates show grotesque figures of humans, animals, and birds. In some designs, warriors appear to be holding severed heads and limbs.

No one knows for certain how the Mississippian people learned about Mexican art. There is no evidence of contact between Central American and Mississippian peoples, such as trade goods or traces of groups moving overland. Artifacts that were clearly made in Mexico have not been found in southern sites. Furthermore, no artifacts or raw materials from North America have been found in Mexico. The strange art of the Temple Mound period continues to puzzle archeologists even today.

At approximately the same time as the Mississippian cultures, other Native Americans were building very different

Mississippian shell ornament from Spiro Mounds, Oklahoma, an example of Southern Temple Mound art. (Stovall Museum of Science and History, University of Oklahoma)

kinds of mounds farther north. Called *effigy* mounds, these are found mostly in Wisconsin and Iowa. Effigy mounds resemble human figures and animals such as bears, hawks, turtles, deer, panthers, and dogs. Though only a few feet high, some stretch over the ground for as much as two hundred feet. Most seem to contain burials, with a few skeletons or bundles of bones placed at key points in the figure such as the head and heart.

Effigy mounds may have been built until sometime during the eighteenth century. Very little, however, is known about the people who made them. These Indians were apparently hunters who left behind only simple stone tools. Yet they had the skill to design and accurately construct complicated shapes that can be seen well only from the air. How did they do it, and why? What do the different animals and birds mean? One idea is that the mounds may have been connected with the Indians' beliefs about certain constellations, particularly the Great Bear, also known as the Big Dipper. A long line of mounds called the Marching Bears is found at Effigy Mounds State Park in Iowa.

The last Indians known to build mounds were the Natchez in Mississippi. These people were studied by the French, who controlled the region in the late seventeenth and early eighteenth centuries. The Natchez villages were grouped around a large temple mound thirty-five feet high and covering seven acres. In each village was a smaller temple mound and another one for the chief's house. Sadly, this final phase in about twenty-five hundred years of mound-building came to a sudden end in 1729. Because of an uprising by the Natchez, the French killed most of the people and drove away the survivors.

The myth of a "super-race" of Mound Builders, who supposedly created great cities many thousands of years ago, has been laid to rest. The people who built the mounds were definitely American Indians. It is not surprising, however, that nineteenth-century Americans thought they must have been someone else, for the artifacts and ways of life of later tribes were very different from those of the mound-building Indians. The fact that the earlier cultures vanished so completely is a riddle in itself.

The mounds, and the people who built them, are still surrounded by mystery. Where did the Adena, Hopewell, and Mississippian peoples come from, and how did they get their ideas? Why did these people put so much energy into creating their immense, complicated earthworks? Why did mound-building cultures flourish, then decline and disappear? By examining the remaining mounds, village sites, and bones of

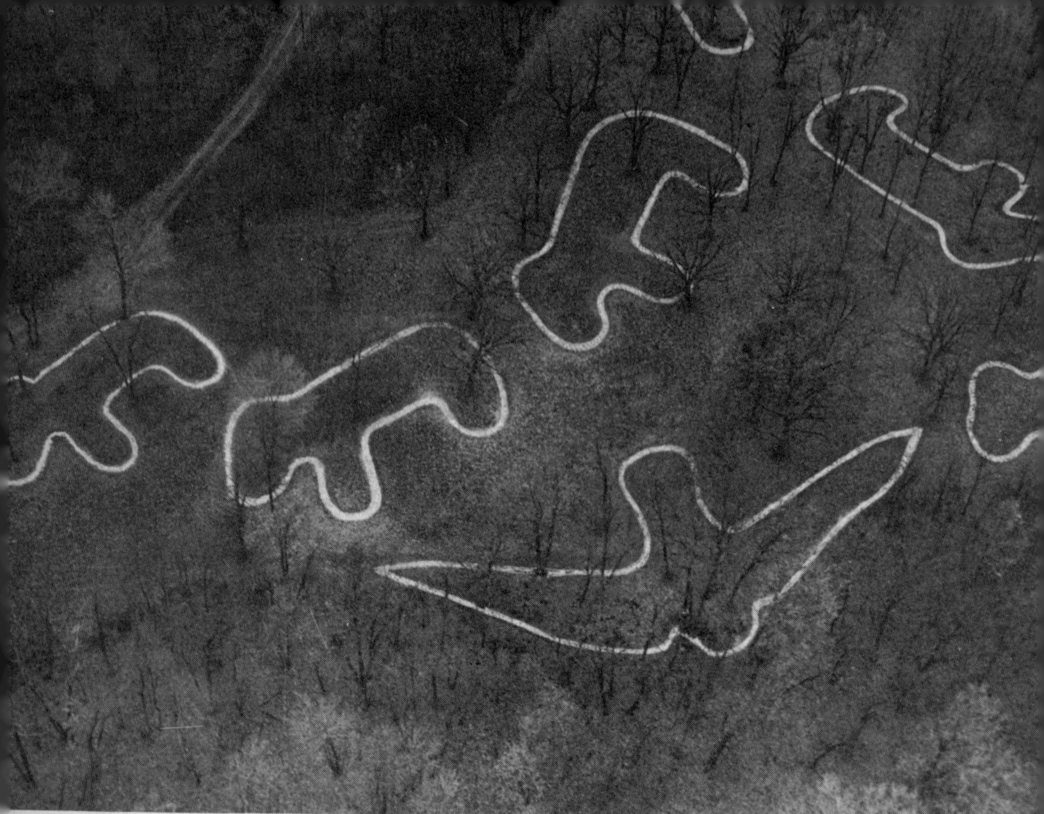

The "Marching Bears" at Effigy Mounds National Monument in Iowa, as seen from the air; the mounds are outlined with lime. (National Park Service)

the people themselves, archeologists are trying to find answers. Slowly the mounds will reveal more of their secrets—and more knowledge about the people who lived in this country long ago.

5

What Became of the Magnificent Hopewells?

INSIDE a mound excavated in the 1920s near Chillicothe, Ohio, archeologists uncovered an incredible sight. The skeletons of two persons, a tall young man and a young woman, lay side by side. At their heads, necks, knees, and wrists were hundreds of fine pearls and copper-covered button ornaments. A line of pearls surrounded the female, and a row of fifty copper ear ornaments lay beside her. The man had worn a necklace of six huge bear teeth, four inches long and set with large pearls. Both skeletons rested on large copper plates, which preserved some fabric, and had foot-long copper rods near the head, possibly for hair braids. In addition, each skull was equipped with a copper nose.

An impressive burial indeed, according to archeologist Henry Shetrone, who excavated and described it. But this was not the only one of such splendor. Like the ancient Egyptians who built pyramids as tombs and buried their rulers with fabulous treasure, the Hopewell people believed in spectacular burials. Their earthworks and grave offerings were the most elaborate of all the mound-building cultures. It was primarily the remains of these people that made nineteenth-century Americans talk about a "super-race" of Mound Builders.

Though archeologists have learned much about them by studying the amazing things they left behind, the "magnificent Hopewells" are still one of the most mysterious peoples of

Hopewell Indians building a mound or earthwork; an artist's conception. (Mound City Group National Monument, National Park Service)

ancient America. Their remains suggest a rich and fascinating culture—yet without written records or accounts, we can never hope to know their full story.

In the 1890s, a group of remarkable mounds were dug open on the farm of Captain Mordecai Hopewell near Chillicothe. They became known as the Hopewell Mounds. Some years later, after finding the same traits in other mounds, archeologists decided that the Indians who had built them formed a particular group, different from the Adena people identified earlier. They adopted the name Hopewell to describe this culture.

Where the Hopewell people came from is a mystery. Like the Adena people before them, they may have moved into Ohio and Illinois from another region, possibly what is now New York State. Most archeologists agree that Hopewell customs seem to have started somewhere around 2400 B.P., probably growing out of the Adena ways. The Hopewell people, however, did everything in a much more extravagant manner.

Although Hopewell and Adena Indians lived near each other for hundreds of years and had many similar customs, little is known about how they got along together. Did they admire, tolerate, or fear each other? Why did they keep their separate ways? We can only wonder. In general, the times seem to have been peaceful, with good relations among different groups of Hopewell, Adena, and the Archaic Indians.

The Hopewell heartland was in central Ohio, in the Scioto River valley south of Columbus. It is there that the mounds were largest and most numerous, and the burials most extravagant. Western Illinois, along the Illinois and Mississippi rivers, was the other most important center. But Hopewell ways were not limited to Ohio and Illinois. They spread far and wide. Sites with Hopewell traits have been found from Minnesota to Florida and Louisiana, from New York State to Kansas. Hopewell settlements were usually located on rivers, which served as highways for trading both goods and ideas.

Archeologists are not sure why Hopewell ways spread to so many parts of the country. Probably simpler tribes were impressed by the Hopewell people's fine crafts, their ceremonies, and their well-organized society. But while some Indian groups adopted Hopewell customs, others did not. Many villages took on certain customs and rejected others. It appears that different Indian groups could pick and choose what they liked about Hopewell culture.

A site is called Hopewell if it reveals certain burial practices and special artifacts. For example, the Hopewell people made many of their most interesting things for ceremonial use and burial. The finest pottery, beautifully decorated, was buried with the dead in the mounds. So were ceremonial weapons such as well-made spear points, stone axe heads, and large knives of obsidian, a glasslike rock. Copper and sheet mica

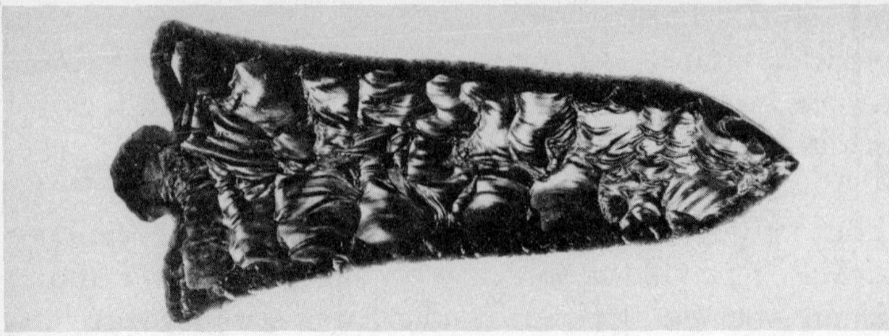

Ceremonial blade of obsidian, found in the Hopewell Mounds near Chillicothe, Ohio. (Ohio Historical Society)

ornaments, shaped like fish or bird claws or human hands, have also been found in mounds.

In one burial, a collection of about two hundred special pipes was discovered. Called platform pipes because the bowl rests on a little platform about four inches long, these stone pipes are outstanding examples of Hopewell art. Beautifully designed and carved with great skill, they resemble a wide variety of birds and animals. No other Indian culture made anything quite like them.

The Hopewell people valued copper highly and used it in many ways, for both tools and decorative objects. Copper breastplates, helmets, beads, buttons, and large ceremonial axes—weighing as much as thirty-eight pounds—have been found in the mounds. The copper was not smelted, but hammered cold into sheets from which the objects were made.

Many of the things buried with the dead were deliberately broken, or "killed," as archeologists say. Possibly this was done so that the spirit of the article might accompany that of its owner. Though many things seem to have been made just to be buried, others had obviously been used in the person's lifetime. For instance, what appear to be "favorite pipes" have been found, worn with handling, broken and repaired.

Probably the most spectacular burials were those with freshwater pearls—hundreds, even thousands of them. They were strung in long necklaces, or sewn on clothes and on bands for arms and ankles. Apparently, pearls sometimes were simply poured on the dead person—in a few cases by the gallon! Most are darkened from being buried in the earth so long, but once they must have been very beautiful.

In some burials, archeologists have found what they call trophy skulls. These are often the skulls of young men, and some are decorated with copper. What was the meaning of such strange grave goods? Were they the remains of important captured enemies, or of honored family members? The answers are not known.

Certain persons, including some women, were given much more elaborate burials than others. The most honored persons were placed at the center of the mound with the largest quantities of valuable and unusual grave offerings. They also appear to have been healthier and taller than others, as archeologists can tell from examining bones and teeth. This

Platform pipe realistically carved to resemble a peregrine falcon. (Ohio Historical Society)

means they probably had better food and an easier life. Though young children were commonly buried in cemeteries or even in trash pits, a few children received honored burials. One baby in an Indiana mound, for example, had hundreds of pearls attached like a fringe to its garment and wore bracelets and anklets of pearls.

Other people, evidently less important, were placed on the sides of the mound or in a second layer. Their grave gifts were less valuable. In some Hopewell communities, especially in Illinois, most of the people seem to have been buried in very low mounds or flat cemeteries.

The honored burials are a good clue to archeologists that the Hopewells had a ruling class. Before the time of the Adena and Hopewell people, American Indians apparently had not divided themselves into social classes. What brought about the change? And who were the most important persons—priests, medicine men, warrior chiefs, or rulers who had come from some other place? Archeologists can only guess. But there is one interesting clue. By studying skulls, archeologists have found that many of the most honored individuals in Ohio mounds had a certain bony growth in their ear canals. Extremely rare, the growth is an inherited condition. This discovery might mean that one particular family ruled Hopewell society over a period of time.

Besides their distinctive grave goods and burials, the Hopewell people left other remarkable creations. The earthworks—huge geometric figures and long artificial ridges—are among the most mysterious of all ancient Indian remains. Most of the Hopewell earthworks are in Ohio, though Mounds State Park in Indiana has unusual fiddle-shaped enclosures and a circle 384 feet across.

Amazing earthworks were built in what is now Newark, Ohio. In the 1840s, a newspaperman named Ephraim G. Squier had a strong interest in the Mound Builders. He made the first careful survey of mounds and earthworks. He called those at Newark as awe-inspiring as "an Egyptian temple."

Ridges of earth up to sixteen feet high formed two huge, almost perfect circles—one twelve hundred feet in diameter—plus an octagon and a square. The geometric figures were connected by long passageways between more ridges. The whole arrangement covered an area of four square miles. The Hopewell people could hardly have made these structures without a good understanding of geometry and engineering. How they acquired the knowledge and skill is a mystery.

What was the purpose of these strange enclosures? Possibly, archeologists think, elaborate ceremonies took place here, with long, majestic processions from one part to another. Perhaps people came from the outlying villages to watch the rulers and priests in their splendor, wearing robes of feathers and buffalo hair, strings of shell beads and pearls, bear and alligator teeth, pendants made from human jaws, and copper helmets with deer antlers attached. All these items have been found in honored burials.

Because the Hopewell people prized such ornaments, they went to great lengths to get the materials needed for them. No alligator teeth, for example, are found in Ohio rivers! Trade networks were therefore organized over an enormous part of the country to obtain the materials that the Hopewells admired so much.

Copper came from mines in the upper peninsula of Michigan. Large sheets of gleaming, nearly transparent mica came from North Carolina. Sharp, black obsidian was brought all the way from Yellowstone, Wyoming. Chunks of iron came from meteors found in Kansas and possibly even as far as Arizona. Many other kinds of stones and minerals, found in different parts of the country, were important in Hopewell trade.

Rare sea shells, alligator teeth, and barracuda jaws were obtained from the Gulf of Mexico and Florida. Chesapeake Bay may have been the source of fossil shark teeth. All these were prized as ornaments. Finished articles, many of them apparently made in the Hopewell centers in Ohio, were also traded among Hopewell groups over a wide area. These items included mica mirrors, conch shells fashioned into drinking cups, and grizzly bear teeth set with pearls.

The Hopewell way of life seems to have been a complicated one. The elaborate ceremonies and burials required great quantities of fine objects, produced by busy artisans who needed valuable materials, which could be obtained only by widespread trade networks. Yet the whole system seems to have worked for a long time. Then, somewhere around A.D. 500 to 700, it came to an end. But why?

Could the luxury-loving Hopewell people have been overcome by sterner, warlike Indians? It does seem as though some kind of unrest, about which very little is known, spread through the northeastern parts of the country at about that period. Near the end of Hopewell times, large earthworks were built on tops of hills and ridges in Ohio. Fort Ancient and Fort Hill near Cincinnati are good examples. These structures look very much like fortresses where large numbers of people could have taken shelter against invaders. Yet some scholars think the large, irregular enclosures were used only for ceremonial purposes. They are still a mystery. Whether the Hopewell people were threatened—and if so, by whom—is not yet known.

A less dramatic cause of Hopewell decline may have been a change in the climate of the midwestern states. That could have brought about changes in the way people lived. In the southeastern part of the country, where the climate remained the same, Hopewell ways lasted longer.

Some archeologists also suggest that, as villages produced more food by better farming methods and hunting weapons such as the bow and arrow, they could have become more independent. This might have made them lose interest in keeping ties with other Hopewell groups. Other archeologists disagree with this idea, saying that corn, the basic crop, was not widely grown until a few hundred years after the decline of Hopewell ways.

Another view is that the complicated trading system began to break down, possibly due to the mysterious period of unrest. This could have caused other big changes in the society. If valuable materials were no longer easily obtained, the craft industries would have dwindled. With fewer luxury goods, the ceremonies and elaborate burials would have become less and less important. Gradually, according to this explanation, the whole Hopewell system would have slowly collapsed.

The picture is still very hazy. But most archeologists and scholars believe that the Hopewell people were not conquered by a barbaric race. Nor did they migrate to a distant land, or die out. Rather, they began to live more simply. Their culture had apparently become as elaborate and complicated as it could. In a sense, there was no way for the Hopewell culture to go but down.

Perhaps, for whatever reasons, the people stopped feeling so strongly about honoring the dead. They lost faith in the importance of mound-building, which used up so much energy and wealth. They no longer wanted to—or no longer could—concentrate on making artistic goods. Perhaps a time came when the common people grew reluctant to serve their rulers. Eventually the Hopewell people had to adopt, willingly or not, the simpler ways of other Indians who had been living in the same region all of this time.

Still, the decline and disappearance of the Hopewell culture remains a baffling question. So, too, is the explanation of these people's exceptional vigor and skills. Their society must have been highly organized to achieve their purposes. But did the Hopewell rulers want something more than luxury, amazing earthworks, ceremonies, and splendid burials? Did they have a vision of a powerful, unified people, like the empires built in other parts of the world? Did they think themselves a kind of "super-race"?

Answers to these and many more questions about the Hopewell people are lost in time.

6

Why Did the Anasazi Leave Mesa Verde?

A LONG-LOST city stands in the southwest corner of Colorado. It is hidden on a beautiful, tree-covered plateau that rises above the plains. Spanish explorers called the plateau Mesa Verde because from a distance it looked like a "green table." They probably never suspected its secrets.

Earlier, Mesa Verde had been full of life. In spite of the sheer cliffs, deep canyons, and scarcity of water, Indian people had lived on the mesa for hundreds of years. Then, for reasons still not clearly understood, the people of Mesa Verde decided to leave their homes. By the year 1300, the place was empty of human life. It was avoided by Indian tribes and unexplored by white settlers until six hundred years later.

One snowy December day in 1888, two young cowboys named Richard Wetherill and Charlie Mason were out searching for stray cattle. They found themselves in the twisting canyons of Mesa Verde. Looking across a valley, the two men saw an amazing spectacle. In the sides of a cliff high above the canyon floor, a whole city of little stone houses appeared to be crammed into an enormous cave. Tiny doorways stared out like eyes.

The cowboys rode around the mesa top until they found an ancient trail that led down to the cave. Exploring some of the crumbling houses, they came across clay pots and stone tools lying just as the owners had left them. They also found ancient corncobs and even some human bones. Thrilled at

Cliff Palace, the largest of the Anasazi cliff dwellings at Mesa Verde. (National Archives)

their discovery of the Cliff Palace, as they called it, the young men went home and told their families.

Wetherill, his four brothers, and Mason showed good sense in exploring the ruins. As amateur archeologists, they found many other cliff dwellings on the mesa and made careful notes. Unfortunately, curiosity-seekers were soon exploring, too. They damaged the cliff dwellings and took fine pottery and other artifacts. To save this amazing place from further damage, Congress declared Mesa Verde a National Park in 1906. Careful archeological work has been carried on there for many decades. Today, Mesa Verde is one of the most important and best known monuments of the ancient peoples of this country.

Who were the mysterious people of Mesa Verde? The nineteenth-century Indians of the area—the Navajo and the Ute—knew about the cliff houses, but they could say nothing about the people who had made them. They called the people *Anasazi,* which means simply "the ancient ones." Archeologists have adopted the name and now use it for the prehistoric

An example of the Basketmakers' craft; some of these baskets were woven tightly enough to hold water. (U.S. Department of Interior, National Park Service)

Indians who lived in the "Four Corners" region—the area where Colorado, Utah, Arizona, and New Mexico meet—from about A.D. 500 to 1300.

The earliest people on Mesa Verde, who seem to have settled there around A.D. 500, probably lived in caves in the cliff sides. Signs of their homes have not been found, however, because later houses were built in the same places. They did not make pottery, but were highly skilled in making baskets, woven tightly enough to hold water. These people carried babies in woven cradles and wrapped dead people in large woven bags. The Wetherill brothers, after finding sites with many fine baskets, called the early people Basketmakers. This name, too, is used by archeologists.

After a while, the Basketmakers must have decided that the mesa top would make a better place to live than their caves in the canyons. Moving up to the flat land, they made houses in the ground. These were round pits about three feet deep. A framework of poles and bark with a thick layer of sun-dried mud covered the pits. An opening in the top served as both smoke hole and entrance. People lived in small clusters of these pit houses all over the mesa top.

It was during this time that the women learned to make pottery, some with beautiful painted designs. The men, meanwhile, were putting more meat in the cooking pots because they were learning to use the bow and arrow. Dogs—and lots of turkeys—lived with the people. A gobbler's main contribution to life on Mesa Verde was its feathers, which were used in weaving. Dog hair was also woven and made into long, beautiful sashes.

Around A.D. 750, the people tried building a different kind of house. These houses were strong, flat-roofed dwellings built of stone slabs held together by clay. Usually several were joined together like a modern apartment house or condominium, and different families lived close together. The name given this type of house is *pueblo,* a Spanish word meaning village.

Circular underground rooms were still made, but gradually lost their purpose as living areas. Instead, the people used them for religious, ceremonial, and even social purposes. Called kivas, the same sort of ceremonial chambers were still being used by the Pueblo Indians of the nineteenth century. Having learned how later Indians used their kivas, archeologists believe that the kivas of the Anasazi probably were used in similar ways. The men of Mesa Verde apparently spent much time in the underground rooms, and the women may have been included in some meetings and ceremonies as well.

The mesa people could not set aside special places for their dead, as did the mound-building Indians. Since space was limited, they buried the dead carefully wherever the soil was soft. Burials have been found in trash pits or abandoned storage pits, under houses, or even in crevasses in the rock.

Because of the dry climate, many bodies were well preserved. Archeologists have been able to learn about the Anasazi people's clothes and even their appearance. The men were about five-feet-four inches tall, the women a few inches shorter. The men wore their hair long, but the women cut off much of theirs and used it for weaving. To keep themselves warm in winter, the people made clothes of hides and rabbit

Courtyard of Spruce Tree House, a cliff dwelling, showing entrances to kivas underground. (U.S. Department of Interior, National Park Service)

fur, and cloaks and blankets of turkey feathers. They also wore ornaments of shell, bone, and turquoise.

The people of Mesa Verde apparently were not threatened by enemies. It would be wrong, however, to think that they led trouble-free lives. On the contrary, they seem to have had a lot of health problems, as archeologists have learned from examining their bones and teeth. A great many babies died, and most of the women lived for only twenty to twenty-five years. The men lived about ten years longer. Almost everyone suffered from arthritis, and bone disease was common. In many skulls found by archeologists, the teeth were worn down to almost nothing. This was probably because the Anasazi ate a lot of cornmeal, ground between pieces of sandstone. The soft stone made the cornmeal full of grit, which wore away the people's teeth as they chewed.

One discovery about the people's appearance puzzled the early archeologists at Mesa Verde. During pueblo-building times, the people began to look quite different from their ancestors. Their heads were shaped differently, unusually broad and flat in back. In fact, at first the archeologists thought another group of Indians had come and settled on the mesa.

Then an answer came to light. The Basketmakers had kept their babies in soft, padded cradles, but the later people strapped their babies to hard boards. As a result, the babies' heads became flattened in back and stayed that way throughout life. The flat heads are still a mystery, however. Why would the people have wanted to do such a thing? Perhaps because everyone came to think a flat, broad head was more attractive!

Around A.D. 1100, the Mesa Verde Indians made another change in the way they lived. They decided to live closer together. Their pueblos grew quite large; some had fifty or more rooms. Many kivas have been found from this period. No longer, however, were the kivas placed just outside the clusters of houses, but instead were right in the middle of the pueblos. Round towers were also built, often attached to the kivas. Thus, the kivas, where people spent so much time, seem to have been given better protection.

This period of large pueblos is sometimes called the golden age of Mesa Verde. But the changes in pueblos and kivas, apparently to make them more compact and secure, suggest something else. Possibly the people were beginning to feel some threat or problem.

Then came a truly dramatic change, sometime around A.D. 1200. Many of the people left the mesa top and moved back down to the cliff sides. The reasons for this change are not clear. One idea is that they moved down to the caves because of religious or superstitious beliefs, but this is only a guess.

The people took their pueblo-building skills with them and, before long, the many large caves in the canyon walls were filled with houses. Most of the population lived in these cliff dwellings. Cliff Palace, the little "city" found by Wetherill and Mason, was the largest, with two hundred rooms and twenty-three kivas.

Scene of daily life in a cliff dwelling, around A.D. 1250. A diorama. (National Archives)

Crops were still grown on the mesa top. Therefore the people had to climb up and down from the cliff houses by ladders, notched poles, and tiny toeholds cut in the rock. It could not have been an easy life, yet the people seem to have expected to live that way for a long time. Though sometimes made hastily, their houses were so solidly built that many have lasted for nearly seven hundred years!

But the Anasazi of Mesa Verde did not stay in the cliff dwellings long. Soon they made another move. This time they decided to pack up and leave the mesa altogether. Though the cliff houses were the most difficult to build, they were lived in for the shortest period of time—only about seventy-five years.

No one is really sure why the Indians of Mesa Verde left the place where their ancestors had lived for hundreds of years. A number of clues, however, may partly explain it.

One clue lies in the way the people changed their type of homes over a period of about two hundred years. They made their pueblos larger, stronger, and better protected—and then they moved down to the caves, which were not easily reached. It certainly looks as though they felt threatened by something.

But there are problems with this theory. No signs of attack, warfare, or other destruction have been found. If there were intruders, archeologists do not know who they might have been. The local Indian tribes first met by white men—the Navajos and Utes—are now believed to have come to the area much later than the thirteenth century. So far as archeologists can tell, there does not seem to have been a particular villain in the mystery of Mesa Verde.

A better clue may be found in the wooden timbers of the houses, such as roof beams. By examining growth rings in the wood of trees cut long ago, archeologists can determine the approximate age of the wood. They can also learn about the climatic conditions that affected the trees while they were growing. This process is called *tree-ring dating*. In years with good rainfall, trees produce wide rings. In dry years, growth rings are narrow. The rings in the wood found in Mesa Verde dwellings reveal that there were severe weather changes from 1276 to 1299. The rains may have come at the wrong time of year for growing crops. More likely, there was a long drought in which crops withered, springs dried up and wildlife died or left the mesa.

The problem, however, may not have been only the long dry period. The Indians had survived many bad droughts before, without having to leave the mesa. Recent studies of the climate of this time suggest another possibility. A period of unusually cold weather set in during the thirteenth century. If the growing season was too short, the people could not produce the food needed for winter.

The gullies and canyons of Mesa Verde reveal another clue. The mesa people built dams in the gullies to hold rainwater. Much soil was washed down and deposited behind these dams, which archeologists have examined. They found that, during the last centuries that people were living on the mesa, much more soil was washed into the gullies than has been washed down since then. This suggests that, because of the farming on the mesa top, the soil was washing away rapidly. As the soil got thinner and less fertile, the people's crops did not grow as well.

One cause of soil erosion was the heavy cutting of trees. The Anasazi had cut trees to clear the mesa top for farming. They also used much wood for fuel and for construction of their houses. As the forest dwindled, not only did soil erosion get worse but game animals left the mesa, meaning less food for the people. The Anasazi of the mesa may have damaged their environment too much. When Mesa Verde was no longer green, people could no longer live on it.

Therefore, life on the mesa during the last years may have been like this. Food was poor and there was little of it. Bad weather and scarce water were continuing problems. Families, uneasy and worried, quarreled and possibly stole from neighbors. People feared that their gods were no longer listening because prayers for rain were not answered. And death came more frequently than ever.

All these problems added up. Starting around 1250, one family after another decided they had had enough. They gathered together whatever they could carry and went away to find someplace better to live. There may have been some other urgent reason that finally forced the people to leave, but if so, it is still unknown.

Did the Indians plan to go back to the mesa when times got better? We shall probably never have an answer to that question. Archeologists do know, however, that not only the people of Mesa Verde were abandoning their homes at this time. Most of the Anasazi of the Four Corners area moved away and found new homes. They apparently went to the southeast, toward the Rio Grande river. There they settled and mingled with other peoples. As time went by, the Anasazi of Mesa Verde—the ancient ones who built cliff palaces—were forgotten.

Today, archeologists continue to study what the people of Mesa Verde left behind. They are trying to understand better what their life on the mesa was like and to unravel the mystery of why it came to an end. Many ruins on the mesa have been left untouched so that future archeologists may be able to study them, using improved methods. Perhaps more clues will be found to help explain what went on in those last years. But for now, visitors to the site can at least have a glimpse of the life that once flourished in the pueblos and fantastic cliff dwellings of Mesa Verde.

7

What Happened to Cahokia, Great City of the Mississippi?

LONG ago, in a proud and wealthy city, a powerful man died and was made ready for the afterlife. A funeral procession carried his body from a great temple to the place of burial. Songs of grief rose to the skies. Priests in rich garments and headdresses performed their ceremonies.

The man was laid on a bed of nearly twenty thousand beads made from rare shells. Many gifts were placed with his body: large rolls of hammered copper, piles of shiny mica, and hundreds of finely made arrowheads. These grave offerings showed his wealth and importance. But it was not only treasure that accompanied the leader to his afterlife.

Four young men were killed. Their heads and hands were cut off, and the bodies placed side by side, arm in arm. Then fifty-three young women were slain. Their bodies, too, were piled in a nearby pit. The priests carried out the last rituals. Then the whole collection of corpses was covered with a mound of earth.

The burial just described was not the only one at this spot. A few other important persons, possibly a ruling family, were also buried in the same place. Some of these, too, were accompanied by rich grave gifts and sacrificial victims. In time, the bodies of several hundred persons were placed there, many in mass graves. The last containers of earth were poured on top. Then the final mound was shaped into a rectangle with a ridged top. But as centuries passed, the graves were forgotten.

Grave gifts of arrowheads buried in Mound 72. Different types may indicate that they were sent from different tribes as tribute. (Illinois State Museum)

The mound, called simply Mound 72 by the archeologists who excavated it, may be seen today. Only six feet high and once more covered by grass, it does not attract much attention. Yet many mysteries linger around this burial place.

Was the important man resting on a bed of shell beads a king, a priest, or merely a very rich citizen? The bones will not tell. Nor can anyone today know whether he was truly admired, or feared and hated. The meaning of the four male bodies—buried carefully, but without heads or hands—is a strange puzzle. And the young women—were they relatives, or wives? Possibly they were killed to prevent the birth of male children who might one day challenge a later ruler. They could even have been captives of war, or sent by other tribes. But whether they were horrified by their fate, or went willingly to death, will never be known.

Mound 72 is only one of many mounds that stand close together near the Mississippi River in western Illinois, eight miles from St. Louis, Missouri. Once there were more than a

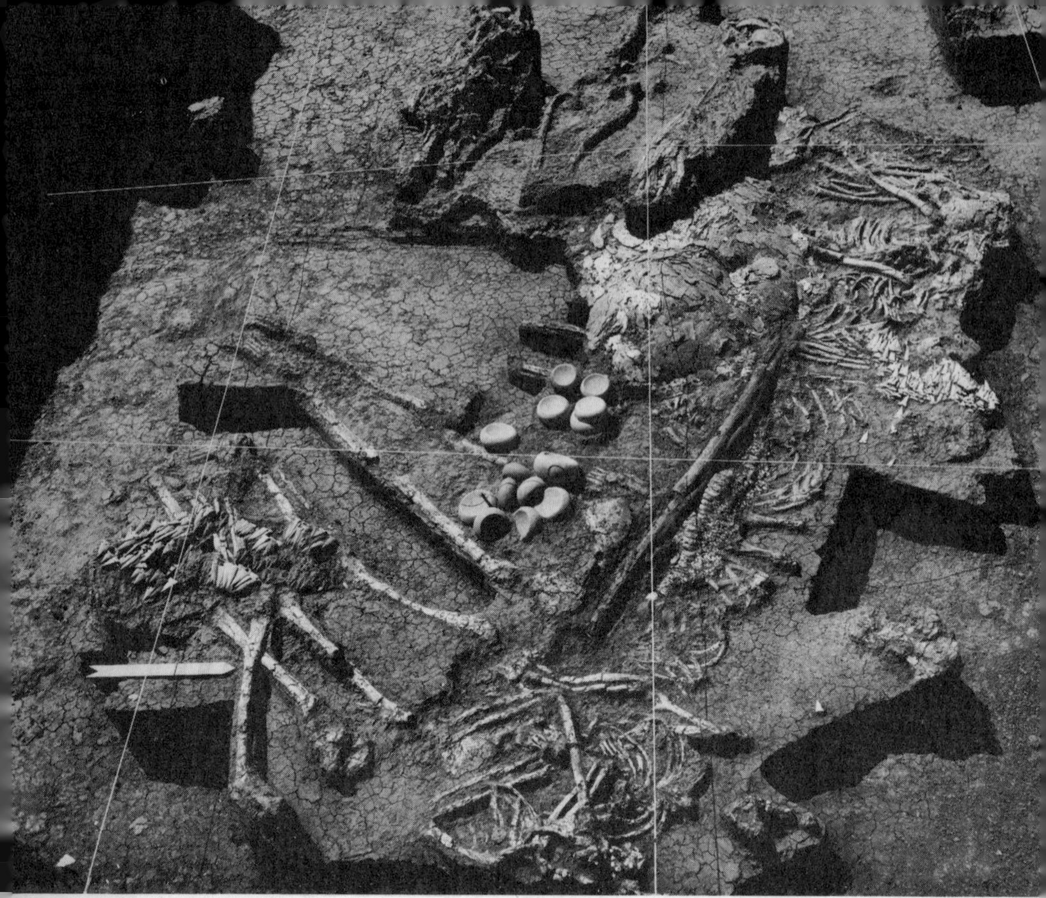

An honored burial at Cahokia Mounds: grave gifts of chunky stones and arrowheads were found in Mound 72 among bones of sacrificial victims. The string grid helps the archeologist record locations of objects. (Illinois State Museum)

hundred mounds at this place, and hundreds more nearby. Some were burial mounds. Most, however, seem to have been built to raise temples, as well as the homes of rulers and other important buildings, above the ground.

The site is called Cahokia Mounds. The name comes from a later Indian tribe living nearby when white men first reached the spot. No one knows what the place was called at the time the mounds were built, or the name of the people who built them. They were part of the Mississippian culture, described earlier.

Cahokia's time of greatest power lasted from around the eleventh to the thirteenth century. For that time, Cahokia was a metropolis, a large, city-like area, with a population of about twenty to thirty thousand people. Up until 1800, no city in this country was larger in population.

Other towns and villages for miles around were connected with Cahokia, much like today's suburbs. The land was fertile and could support many people. With the Mississippi and the Missouri rivers nearby, the people of Cahokia carried on trade with other Indians in places from northern Michigan to the Gulf of Mexico. Archeologists know this because of the artifacts found at the site. The valuable grave offerings in Mound 72, for example, came from places far away. Possibly they were sent by distant tribes as tribute.

The most awesome sight at Cahokia today is the great mound at the center of the area. Rising to a height of one hundred feet, it is one of the largest man-made creations of earth in the world. The base measures 1,080 by 710 feet and covers nearly fifteen acres—about an acre more than the Great Pyramid of Egypt. On the summit stood a huge temple, as large as a basketball court and possibly forty to fifty feet high.

This mound is called Monks Mound because of a group of European monks who briefly settled nearby and farmed on it early in the nineteenth century. From ground level, the eroded sides of the mound make it look like a small hill. Anyone who has climbed the 146 wooden steps to the top, however, and looks far out over the countryside, realizes what a huge creation it is. In the mound's days of glory, a ramp led up to the top. Processions to and from the temple on the summit must have been an amazing sight.

Monks Mound was built in stages over a period from A.D. 900 to 1150. Archeologists believe, however, that it was left unfinished. From 1150 on, only smaller mounds were built. Whether this was due to a need to save soil and labor, or due to a change in the people's beliefs, remains a riddle.

How was such a colossal mound built? Like every other Indian mound in this country, Monks Mound was built entirely by hand. The people had no animals to carry loads of

Monks Mound, about 100 feet high and 1080 feet long; this huge mound, like all other Indian earthworks, was built by basketsful of earth. (Illinois State Museum)

soil. They had not invented wheels, and therefore had no carts. Their tools were simple hoes and shovels made of stone or large shells. Their only earth-moving power was their own muscles. They built Monks Mound by digging and dumping basketful after basketful of soil. The borrow pits—places from which the soil was taken—were about half a mile away.

Archeologists know this much. But how the men, women, and children of Cahokia were organized and persuaded to do the work is not understood. We probably will never know whether they worked gladly, or were forced to labor under threat of punishment.

Why the Cahokian way of life declined and disappeared, archeologists can only guess. Traces of what was once a large stockade are now being studied. This may hold some clues to what finally happened to the great metropolis of Cahokia.

The early centuries of life at Cahokia seem to have been peaceful. Starting in the twelfth century, however, the rulers decided to build a stockade. This stout, solid barrier measured about two miles around. Three times, over the years, it was replaced. Many defensive towers were built on it, as archeologists can tell from the position and greater size of the holes where the posts stood.

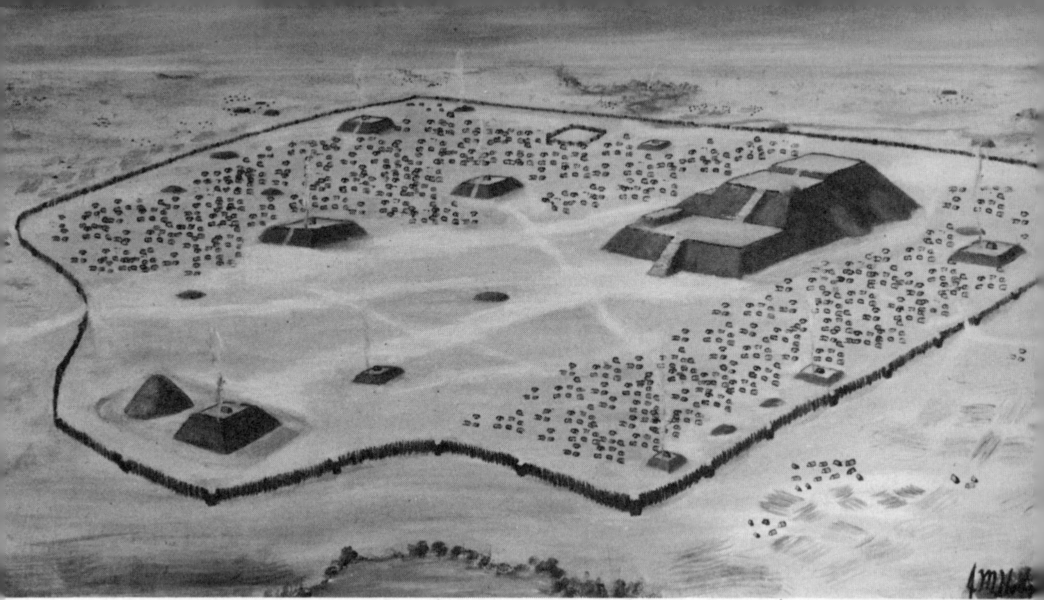

The great ceremonial center at Cahokia as it may have appeared around A.D. 1200; an artist's conception. (Illinois State Museum; artist, J. Michael Hodges)

Perhaps the stockade was needed because of the growing size and importance of the ceremonial area. It could have been intended to hide the important mounds from the common people. Usually, however, a stockade is for protection against an enemy. But who could have been threatening such a powerful city? Archeologists can only speculate. Possibly the danger came from wandering tribes, or from the smaller towns and villages uniting against the central city. The threat might even have been inside Cahokia. The idea of a rebellion, with the common people rising up against the ruling classes, is not impossible. No clue, however, has yet been found as to who the enemy was or whether attacks were ever made.

The stockade suggests something more. The barrier was built of heavy logs placed in a solid row. Each new stockade required from twelve thousand to fifteen thousand large trees, or more. That would have used up some of the nearby forests and damaged the natural environment. Game animals and birds would have become fewer, and soil erosion would have taken place.

The soil may also have become less fertile simply from producing so much corn for so many people. Archeologists also think there may have been some changes in climate starting around A.D. 1250. This would have affected the growing season, leading to shortage of food. Perhaps groups of people, discontented, started moving away to land that had been less heavily used. Then, without a large population to support them, the ruling class of priests and chiefs at Cahokia would gradually have lost power. Like the Hopewell culture, after a while the old way of life would have broken down.

The decline of Cahokia, archeologists believe, probably came from such causes rather than from violent changes. All that is known for certain, however, is that at about this time, other communities along the Mississippi River were starting to grow. By 1500, Cahokia was abandoned.

The mounds of Cahokia still hide many secrets. Some will never be found, because much of the site has been destroyed in the past by farming and by more recent highway construction. Archeologists have excavated only about one percent of the remaining area. Thus years of painstaking work lie ahead before we know much more about Cahokia in its glory and its decline.

Meanwhile, the awesome Monks Mound still looms above the plain. Though it, too, is in danger of erosion and slumping, it stands like a monument to a once-great city, or like a tomb, concealing truths about a vanished people.

8

Sun Spirals, Woodhenges, Medicine Wheels— What Did They Mean?

HIGH on a bare, windswept mountaintop in northern Wyoming lies an unusual circle of stones, about eighty feet across. In the center, more rocks are gathered into a pile called a *cairn.* Twenty-eight lines of stones lead from the center cairn to the edge of the circle, like spokes of a wheel. Just outside the circle stand six smaller cairns.

Many, many small circles of stones have been found on the Great Plains. Most were used to anchor Indian tepees, and others may have been monuments to dead chiefs. The large circle in the Bighorn Mountain range in Wyoming, however, apparently had a different purpose. It is called a medicine wheel—"medicine" meaning magic or spiritual—and is the largest one ever found.

The Bighorn Medicine Wheel is difficult to reach, high in the mountains where heavy snow can fall even in June. For a long time no one understood its meaning. In the nineteenth century, when white men asked the local tribes about the wheel, the Indians said little. "The sun built it," they explained, "to show us how to make a tepee."

In the 1920s, a scholar suggested that the medicine wheel could have had something to do with Indian sun rituals. Its design looked like the floor plan of a special wooden building made by the Cheyenne for their sun dance at the start of summer. But which came first: the wheel or the sun dance house? No one could say for certain.

Bighorn Medicine Wheel as it appeared in the 1920s. Today a fence surrounds the site. (Archives–American Heritage Center, University of Wyoming)

John Eddy, an astronomer in Boulder, Colorado, also thought the wheel had something to do with the sun. He wondered whether it could have been designed to indicate certain times in the solar year. In 1972 and 1973, Eddy studied the wheel carefully at the time of the summer *solstice.* The summer solstice usually takes place on June 21 and is often called the first day of summer. On this day, the longest of the year, the sun rises on the horizon at the point farthest north in its yearly travels.

At dawn of that day, Eddy stood by one of the cairns just outside the wheel. From there, he observed that the center cairn lined up almost exactly with the sunrise. This line-up, called an alignment, took place only at the summer solstice. In addition, Eddy observed that other cairns indicated the points on the horizon where, on certain days, three bright stars appeared at dawn. They shone very briefly, almost like a flash, just before the sun brightened the sky. One rose shortly before the summer solstice, one rose twenty-eight days after the solstice, and the third, twenty-eight days later. The twenty-eight spokes in the wheel may have helped in keeping track of those periods of time.

Why would the people who made the medicine wheel have wanted to know when the solstice and the star risings occurred?

People have always watched the sky and wondered. The sky is a mysterious place, full of sights that are difficult to understand. Gazing at the stars, they would make up stories to try to explain those tiny lights. From time to time, they watched the moon—or even the sun—disappear in an eclipse, and many probably trembled with fear. As winter approached and the days grew shorter and darker, they must sometimes have worried. The sun seemed to be going away. Would it return? Or could something go wrong with the heavens?

American Indians, who lived so close to nature, felt a strong connection with their environment, the earth and the sky. They wanted to understand the world, for they needed to feel sure that everything would continue in the normal manner. One way they tried to learn about the world was by keeping track of the movements of the sun, moon, and stars. This knowledge helped them to predict the changing seasons.

Today, some archeologists are learning about the ways in which people of the past observed the skies. These archeologists often work with astronomers. Together they have developed a new field of study called *archeo-astronomy.* In many parts of this country, archeo-astronomers have examined sites where Indians once observed the movements of heavenly bodies. They even call these places astronomical observatories. Several different kinds have been discovered. The Bighorn Medicine Wheel, with its alignments for the summer solstice and the star risings, appears to be one.

With the help of observatories, American Indians kept track of the changing seasons and watched for certain signs in the heavens that must have had special meanings for them. What those meanings were, archeologists can only guess.

Nothing is known, for example, about the Indian people who made the Bighorn Medicine Wheel. As for when it was made, there are almost no clues. A few beads, broken pieces of pottery called *sherds,* and a piece of wood found in a cairn all date from about two hundred years ago. They could, however, have been left there long after the wheel was made.

With two archeologists, astronomer John Eddy studied another medicine wheel, in Saskatchewan, Canada. The cairns of this wheel, called Moose Mountain Medicine Wheel, are placed like those of the Bighorn Wheel and seem to show approximately where the same three bright stars rise.

The points on the horizon where stars rise, however, change slightly over long periods of time. Therefore, Eddy figured out when, in the past, the three bright stars rose closest to the points indicated by the cairns. With this information, he estimated that the Moose Mountain Wheel may have been made sometime around the start of the Christian era.

Then the archeologists did their part of the research. Under one cairn they found tiny bits of charcoal. When tested by the radiocarbon method, the charcoal gave a date sometime around 440 B.C. This finding seemed to confirm Eddy's estimate. The archeo-astronomers concluded that the wheel was made approximately two thousand years ago. If the Bighorn wheel was made at about the same time, then it, too, is close to two thousand years old—rather than two hundred!

But why did people need an astronomical observatory in the high mountains? Archeologists have always thought that, in prehistoric times, only farmers needed to keep close track of the seasons, since they had to know the best times of year to plant seeds. The Indians of the Plains, however, were wandering hunters, not farmers.

Possibly the people wanted to know when the summer solstice occurred because it had important religious meaning for them. Something like this may have taken place: In late spring one or two important persons, such as medicine men, went up the difficult trail to the medicine wheel. There, for several days they watched the sunrises in the chilly dawn. At last the sun rose at the right spot in line with the two cairns. The medicine men believed it a sacred vision. They then returned to their people, declaring that the heavens were in order and it was time for an important ceremony, perhaps the start of a new year.

In addition to the religious purposes, the wheel may have had some practical uses. Two months after the summer solstice, when one of the bright stars rose at dawn, it could have been understood as a warning that the short summer was nearly over. The hunters would then have known it was time to come down from the high mountains and prepare for winter.

These scenes suggest ways in which the Plains Indians could have used the wheel. There are other possible reasons why they may have wanted to keep track of the passing days. For instance, the buffalo herds, on which they depended, migrated at certain times of the year. By watching for the rising of particular stars, the Indians may have known when it was time for the buffalo to come near.

Still, archeo-astronomers can only speculate about what the wheel meant for these people of the past. Europeans—Spanish explorers—first came to the Plains in the sixteenth century. The Indians' way of life began to change soon thereafter. They learned to keep horses and therefore could move around more easily, following the buffalo herds instead of waiting for the animals to come at a particular time. After a while, the information revealed by the medicine wheel may no longer have been needed so much. The people, though still believing it to have some religious importance, gradually forgot what the wheel once meant.

One fact seems clear. The Indians who built the medicine wheels, by carefully observing their world, invented an accurate device to keep track of passing time. In some way, that knowledge played an important part in their lives.

The word *henge,* which actually means a circular earthen enclosure, can also be used to describe an arrangement of standing objects such as tall stones. Stonehenge in England is the most famous example. Woodhenge, a site that once had circles of wooden posts, also exists in England. Now archeologists are finding that woodhenges were built in the central part of the United States.

At the great city and ceremonial center of Cahokia in Illinois are traces of more than one woodhenge. Post pits have been found for parts of four large, carefully constructed circles, built probably between eight and nine hundred years ago. The circles overlap and are from 210 to 480 feet in diameter. Archeologist Warren Wittry, believing that they might have been intended for observing the sun, excavated Cahokia's woodhenges in the 1960s and 1970s.

A woodhenge can be reconstructed and studied fairly easily. Dr. Wittry set up a high observation post at the center of one of the circles. Three other large posts were placed at what he believed were key points in the circle. At the summer solstice, Wittry found, the center post and one of the circle posts lined up with the rising sun. Another alignment occurred at the winter solstice, the shortest day of the year, around December 21.

Between the center post and the third post in the circle, an alignment could be seen at the fall and spring *equinoxes.* These are the two times of year, around September 21 and March 21, when daylight and nighttime are equal in a twenty-four-hour time period.

Astronomer-priests probably designed these woodhenges, Wittry says, and went to them at certain times of the year to observe the sun's movements. Their ability to predict the changes in season gave them prestige and possibly made them appear to have special powers.

The circles of posts, besides marking important days of the year, may also have been a sort of sacred space. Possibly ceremonies—and other strange activities—were held in them. Excavation near certain post holes turned up a few

An artist's conception of the woodhenge near Kansas City. Markings on the small stone in the inset may be a clue to the way the observatory was used. (Artist, Cathy Johnson; first appeared in *Science Digest,* © 1982 by the Hearst Corporation)

human bones. Were parts of bodies, Wittry wonders, hung on the posts in some kind of ritual? These woodhenges may hold many clues about the people of Cahokia and their beliefs.

Another site was discovered near Kansas City, Missouri, when plans were under way for the creation of a lake. Archeologists studying the land came across an unusual series of post mold marks. Post mold is the soil that forms where a wooden post has rotted away in the ground, a little different in color from the surrounding soil.

The post mold marks formed a nearly perfect square. Each side of the square was about thirty-five feet long. It looked like the traces of a large building, perhaps a fort. But where the corners should have been, there were no post marks, and the south side of the square had a double row of them. A small triangle of posts once stood in the center.

To test a hunch, members of the Kansas City Astronomy Society made a simple reconstruction of the square. At different times of the year in 1982–83, they observed the sunrise at this reconstructed square. On the summer solstice, a person standing a certain distance from the center poles could see the sunrise and sunset through two of the open corners. At the winter solstice, from a particular spot, the sunrise and sunset could be seen through the other two corners.

The square also showed the spring and autumn equinoxes. On those days, the rising sun shone right between the double row of posts. The hunch was correct: The mysterious square of wooden posts appears to have been a solar observatory. Therefore, although a square rather than a circle, it is now being called a woodhenge. A stone found at the site, marked by curious straight lines and geometric shapes, may hold clues to the way the observatory was used. Archeologists believe the people who created this woodhenge lived around one thousand years ago and had some connection with Cahokian culture.

The remains of the Kansas City woodhenge cannot be studied further, for they are now covered by the man-made lake. A permanent reconstruction has been built nearby for visitors to see, but the secrets of how the people used their woodhenge, and how they understood the information it revealed, are locked in the past.

A very different kind of observatory stands in the sun-baked desert of northwestern New Mexico. Whereas woodhenges and medicine wheels line up with the sun at the times of its rising or setting, this device uses the sun only at midday.

In Chaco Canyon, once the home of Anasazi people like those of Mesa Verde, a rock rises more than four hundred feet from the desert floor. Called Fajada Butte, it has some Indian

The three slabs of stone at the Fajada Butte sun marker. (© 1978, Solstice Project, Inc.; photographer, Karl Kernberger)

petroglyphs. In late June of 1977, an artist named Anna Sofaer visited the butte to study the rock art. By noon she had climbed nearly to the top. As she examined some carvings, she observed a curious pattern of sunlight and shadow on the rock face. It was caused by an unusual rock formation.

Three large slabs of stone, each about nine feet high and one foot thick, had fallen from the rock above. Side by side and only a few inches apart, they stood on end. Their narrow sides leaned at an angle against the rock face, which was in shadow. Two spirals had been cut in the shaded rock, the larger spiral measuring about thirteen by sixteen inches. Small patches of sunlight on the spirals were what held Anna Sofaer's attention.

The next spring, Sofaer returned to Chaco Canyon with two other persons who were interested in Indian astronomy. Day after day, they climbed the butte and patiently watched the pattern of sunlight on the shadowed rock behind the three slabs. Near noon, around the day of the summer solstice, something dramatic happened. The rock face was in shadow—until a small spot of bright sunlight fell upon the top of the larger spiral. Slowly the spot moved straight downward, taking the form of a dagger. It passed exactly over the center of the spiral, and then disappeared.

In the days that followed, the downward path of the "dagger of light" changed. Gradually it moved to the right of the spiral's center. Another, smaller spot of light was meanwhile appearing to the left of the larger spiral.

Sofaer and her companions returned to Fajada Butte at other times of the year to observe the sunlight on the spirals. At the fall equinox, the second streak shone on the center of the smaller spiral. In the following days it, too, moved to the right. Three months later came the winter solstice. On that day, the two streaks of light passed on either side of the large spiral. Thus, in winter the spiral seemed to be completely without light, as if it was a symbol of the cold days when the sun shines for the briefest time. From then on, the light streaks appeared in reverse order. Slowly they moved to the left until the next summer solstice. Then the single "dagger" once again struck the exact center of the spiral.

This beautiful and fascinating sun device is still clouded by mystery. How much of it was made by human beings? And what meaning did it have for its creators?

The spirals, of course, were carefully carved for a definite purpose. But the vertical stone slabs could have simply fallen into place from the rock above. There are other spots in Chaco Canyon where slabs of stone have broken off and fallen to rest in odd positions. A number of archeo-astronomers and geologists have studied the site. Most believe that the heavy slabs of stone were not set in place on purpose. According to

The "dagger of light" on the larger spiral, near noon at the time of the summer solstice. (© 1978, Solstice Project, Inc.; photographer, Karl Kernberger)

this view, the creators of the spirals apparently discovered a curious pattern of light on the rock face and then turned it into a sun marker by carving the spirals.

Other people, including Anna Sofaer, have felt certain that the whole sun marker was designed and constructed deliberately, including the careful placement of the slabs. They have argued that each part of the solar device—slabs, rock face, spirals—is too exact for any part of it to have been accidental. If one part were changed, everything would be thrown off.

More recent studies of the site, however, suggest that the sun marker is not extremely accurate. Because the daily changes in the sun's path are very small around the time of the solstices, changes in the streaks of sun are too slight to indicate the precise days of the solstices. Pueblo Indian methods of observing the solstices by seeing the sun rise at the horizon are, in fact, more accurate. This argument supports the view that the placing of the rock slabs was, in fact, accidental.

Therefore, some archeo-astronomers suggest that the sun marker was probably not intended as a scientific calendar, but for some different purpose. Rather than predicting certain days with accuracy, it could have served as a shrine where priests went at times to celebrate important events in the year. But this is still speculation. No one is really sure why the Anasazi wanted to observe the changing paths of the "daggers of light."

Sun spirals, woodhenges, medicine wheels . . . we will never know the full story of what they meant for their creators. Every year, however, archeo-astronomers discover more about the clever ways in which people of the past observed the movements of the sun, moon, and stars. Long, long ago, American Indians were trying to make sense of the mysterious universe. Only now are we learning to appreciate their achievements.

9

What Are the Secrets of Mystery Hill?

A NEW ENGLAND villager named Jonathan Pattee got in trouble with the law around the year 1826. Running away, he found a place to hide on a lonely hilltop near North Salem in southern New Hampshire. The land was stony and poor, a strange place to settle down, and Pattee was not a young man. Nevertheless, he and his wife, with some of their thirteen children, apparently tried to do some farming on the hillside. In 1848, Pattee died, and a few years later the house was destroyed by fire. Today no trace remains of the Pattee house or farm.

Yet people still remember Jonathan Pattee. The story—or legend—persists because of one very surprising thing about that Yankee farmer. He apparently spent his spare time building caves. That, at least, is what the local legends say.

All over the top of the wooded hill where Pattee lived stands a strange collection of half-ruined stone huts, tunnels, walls, and huge rocks resting at odd angles. Everything is built of rough stones tightly fitted together without mortar or cement. There seems to be no design or purpose to the place.

One large structure, near the center of all the stone walls and chambers, is full of surprises. It looks like a tunnel built against a huge split boulder. The upper part of the tunnel has two branches, giving the structure a T shape. Massive slabs of rock form the roof. Inside, on one of the stone walls, is a crude drawing of a running deer. A stone seat projects into

Sketch of the stone chambers at Mystery Hill, as the site appeared in the 1930s. (First appeared in *New England Quarterly,* September 1939)

the passageway in one place, and several large niches are built into the walls. One is large enough for a person to hide in, unseen—and, through a small hole, be able to watch the passageway.

Close to this strange niche, a narrow tunnel leads like a tube to the outside. It ends under a large, flat slab of stone, which rests on four smaller stones. This slab measures about nine feet by six and weighs around four and one-half tons. A rectangular groove has been cut in it, leading off the stone at one end. The slab looks like a place where sacrifices might have taken place, the groove channeling blood or other liquid. Hence it is now called the Sacrificial Table. There seems to be a connection between this stone, the hollow tube, and the large niche where a person could hide, as if a voice might come from the ground at the spot where sacrifices were being made. This idea gives the whole structure the name by which it is currently called, the Oracle Chamber.

Why would Jonathan Pattee, when not busy milking cows or splitting wood like any other hard-working farmer, have wanted something like an Oracle Chamber? Why did he need

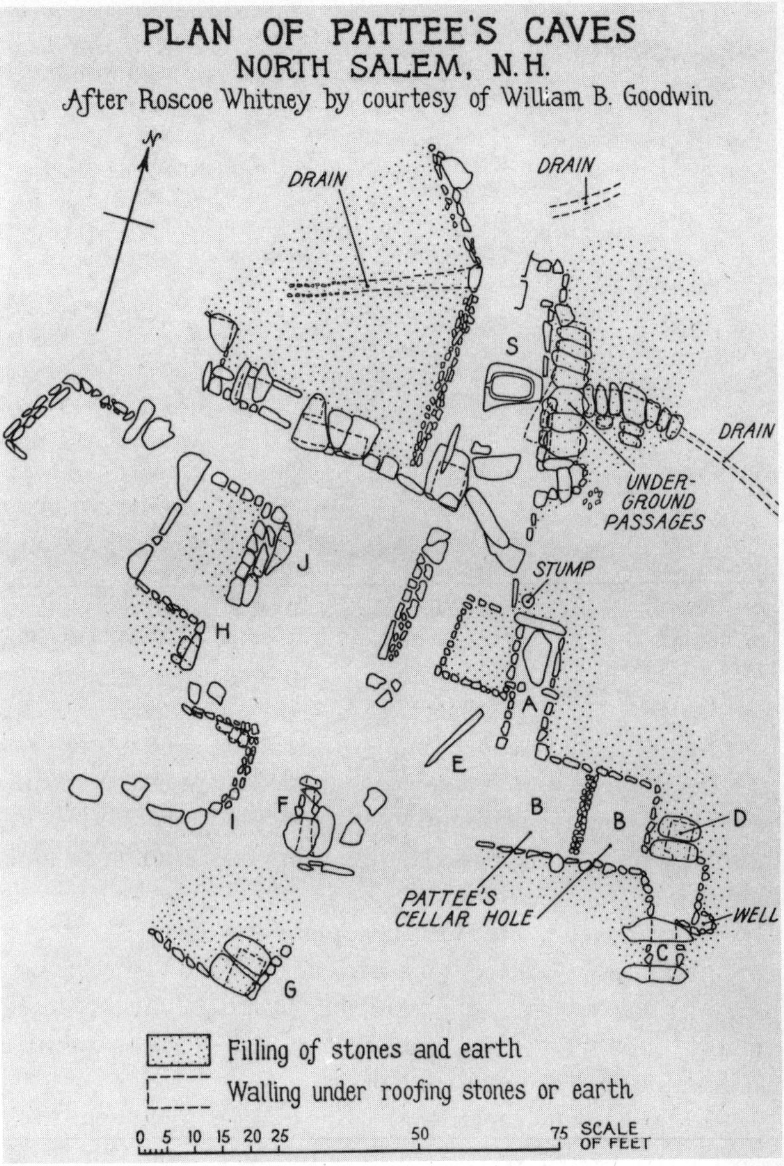

Plan of the stone chambers drawn in the 1930s. Letters on different features correspond to the letters in the sketch; S indicates the Sacrificial Table next to the Oracle Chamber. (First appeared in *New England Quarterly*, September 1939)

The Sacrificial Table . . . What was its true purpose? (Photographer, Duane W. Eichholz)

a Sacrificial Table? Was it simply for making lye for soap, or crushing apples for cider, as some people have said? Why did he make his stone walls in such a crazy pattern? Why, in short, did he want to build that amazing cluster of caves and tunnels?

For many years the local people have given a simple explanation for "Pattee's Caves," as they call the place. Jonathan Pattee was an eccentric, a kind of crackpot. A number of archeologists and scholars still agree with this explanation, but not everyone does.

In 1937, a wealthy man who was interested in ancient sites bought the property. He studied the caves and did some excavating. Convinced that the hill was settled a thousand years ago by Irish monks who had escaped from Vikings, he called the place "The Stone Village." His ideas about the Irish monks caused much excitement at the time. An archeologist from Harvard University, who was an expert on ruins in Ireland, went to study the site. He was unable to find anything at all that looked Irish and decided the "eccentric farmer" explanation was probably the most reasonable.

He made one discovery, however, that raised puzzling questions. A rotted pine stump was found next to a wall, its roots entangled in the stonework. The archeologist knew from this that it had grown after the wall was built. He figured that the tree must have started growing in the late seventeenth or early eighteenth century. Therefore, he said, some of the stone structures probably were there before Pattee settled on the hill. But he couldn't say who had built them—unless it was another farmer.

In 1955, two archeologists connected with Yale University and the American Museum of Natural History worked on the site. They found only artifacts from the nineteenth and twentieth centuries, such as broken dishes and nails. They agreed that Pattee had probably built the stone chambers.

At that point, unfortunately, most archeologists and historians seem to have lost interest in the place. If those caves were just the vegetable cellars and chicken coops of a half-crazy farmer, they argued, why bother to excavate them?

The site does present problems for archeologists. Because it is so large, decisions about where to excavate are difficult. Moreover, the man who had hoped to prove that it was built by Irish monks dug into the ruins carelessly. He may also have tried to do some reconstruction, although no one seems to know exactly what or how much he did. But even before that, a far worse attack had been made. In the second half of the nineteenth century, the site was used as a quarry! Builders took away great quantities of the stone to nearby towns for bridge foundations and street curbs. Possibly as many as half of the huge slabs were lost in this way.

No explanation for the site has yet been found on which everyone can agree. Many people still believe that Pattee built the stone chambers and walls. Yet a visitor to this amazing place will wonder how Jonathan Pattee could have managed the job. It is hard to imagine a poor farmer, even a half-crazy one, moving all those tons of stone entirely by himself. It is also hard to suppose that he found someone else, equally crazy, to help him. But if not Pattee, then who did make those structures? "Mystery Hill" is what the place has been called in recent years, and for good reason.

The site's present owners have taken many steps to preserve it. A few limited archeological studies have been made. Bits of charcoal found in certain walls have been dated by the radiocarbon method. They appear to be as old as three to four thousand years. Another recent discovery is an old quarry on one side of the hill. Huge blocks of stone, up to fifteen feet long, have been partially removed from the bedrock. They were cut by methods using fire and wedges. Whoever was quarrying here evidently had no metal tools.

Mystery Hill is, in fact, far more than a collection of strange chambers. Low stone walls wander all over the hilltop. Set among them are approximately seventy large stones, three to five feet tall. Most are a triangular shape, obviously formed by human hands, not by nature. Some have fallen, and others still stand or have been recently set up again.

In the 1970s, archeo-astronomers examined these stones. They found that several have solar alignments. Standing at a particular spot near the center of the site, a person can see that certain stones point to the sunrise and sunset at the winter and summer solstices. Others are aligned with the sun at the spring and fall equinoxes. One group of stones points to the North Star. Directly opposite, at the other side of the site, is a stone wall that indicates south. Other stones mark the sunrise on May 1 and November 1, important festival days in ancient Europe, which may have some connection with our May Day and Halloween.

One thing is clear about Mystery Hill. It was planned partly as an astronomical observatory and is, in fact, a very complicated one. For this reason the present owners of the site now call it "America's Stonehenge," comparing it with the famous circles of stones in England, constructed about five thousand years ago.

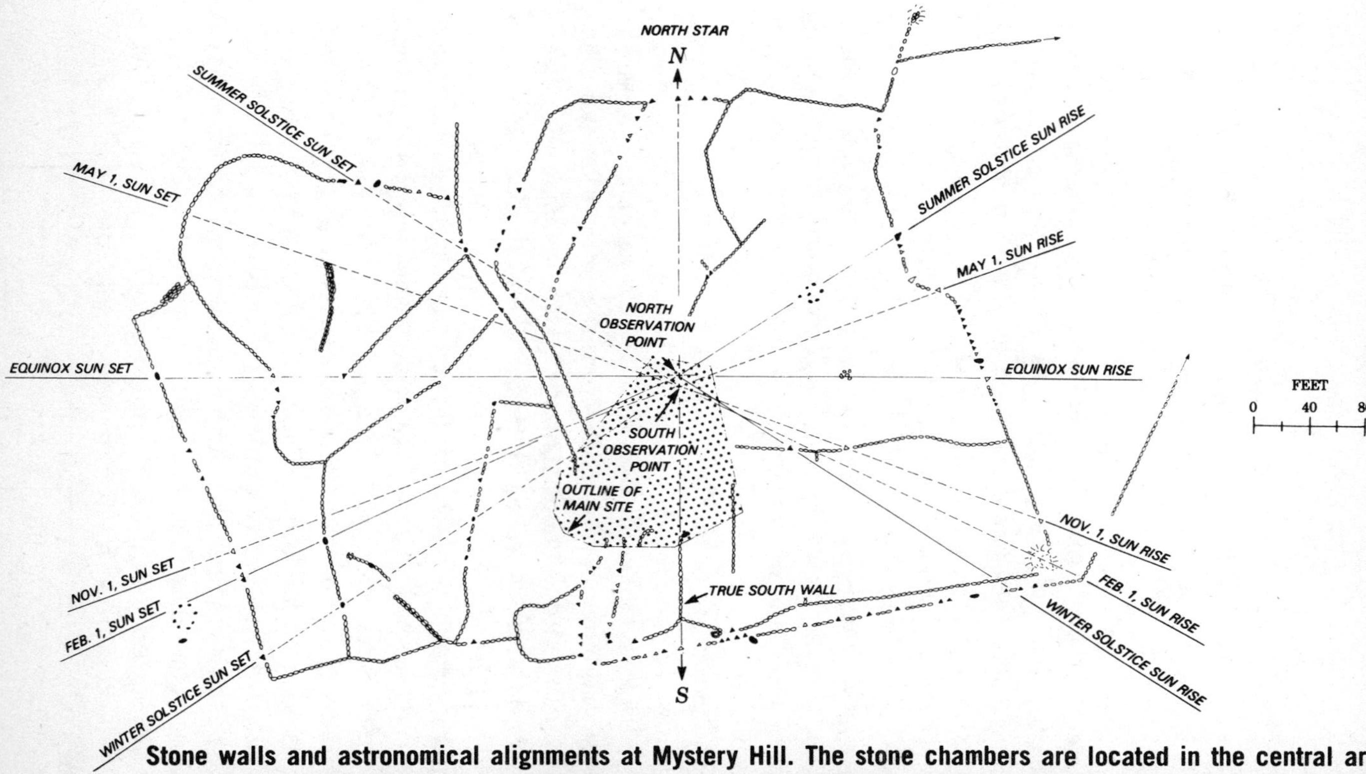

Stone walls and astronomical alignments at Mystery Hill. The stone chambers are located in the central area called "main site." (Map by Daniel J. Leary, based on survey information by G. Pearsons Associates, Derry, N.H.)

But Mystery Hill is not the only place of its kind. In many parts of New England and New York, there are sites with stone chambers and large standing stones similar to those of Mystery Hill. Some of the large stones set in the ground seem to have astronomical alignments. One site in Vermont, for example, has also been carefully studied by archeoastronomers.

In some places, the stone arrangements look like ancient sites in Europe. This raises another theory about who could have constructed the chambers and standing stones. Some people think they may have been left by Celts who came to this continent about four thousand years ago.

The question remains: Who made such places as Mystery Hill? Were they ancient Celts, Irish monks, or eccentric Yankee farmers? Whoever they were, it appears that they lived all over New England. Perhaps, however, we do not have to look for answers so far away in time and place as the Bronze Age Celts of Europe. Clues about Mystery Hill may be found closer to home.

As we have seen, American Indians in many parts of this country found different ways to observe the sun and the skies. Why couldn't they also have set up the sun-marker stones in New Hampshire? For that matter, why couldn't they have built all the structures at Mystery Hill and similar sites?

If Mystery Hill was the work of American Indians, there are still many baffling questions. Little can even be guessed about who those people were, or when and how they lived. Whether they were different from other Archaic Indians who lived in New England from one thousand to five thousand years ago, no one knows for certain. Why did they build the puzzling chambers and tunnels and walls? How did they use the Oracle Chamber and the Sacrificial Table? No clues have yet been found to these riddles.

Those who built the rock structures on the hilltop at North Salem are still a "mystery people." Only after archeologists can study the place carefully will more light fall on the many secrets of Mystery Hill.

10

Who Left Those Cannons on the Beach?

ENGLAND and Spain were enemies in the sixteenth century. Spain had grown rich from conquests in the New World, and England wanted some of that wealth. Therefore, the bold English sea captain Francis Drake was always on the lookout for treasure-laden Spanish galleons. When he met one, he usually came out the winner.

In 1578, Drake sailed around South America, seizing treasure from Spanish ships and settlements along the way. By the time he reached the west coast of North America, his ship, *The Golden Hind*, was filled with tons of gold and silver. In hopes of finding a shorter way home to England, Drake sailed a long distance up the coast of California, searching for a passage. But his ship had sprung leaks and was overladen with treasure. He had to turn back.

Someone on board *The Golden Hind*—tradition says it was the ship's chaplain—wrote a detailed account of the voyage. According to this report, Drake headed back down the California coast and eventually found safe harbor where he could make repairs. The crew unloaded the treasure, arms, and the ship's eighteen cannons. Then the vessel was tipped over on its side on the beach. The men stayed at this place for five weeks in the summer of 1579, cleaning and repairing the bottom of the ship. They built a simple fort for protection, but were never in danger. Instead, the local Indians welcomed the Englishmen with great excitement and honors.

Captain Francis Drake and his men being welcomed by Indians on the coast of California in 1579. (From De Bry's *Grand Voyages, America*, 1599. Courtesy of the National Maritime Museum, London)

Drake claimed the land in the name of his queen, Elizabeth I. He called it Nova Albion—Nova meaning "new" and Albion being an old name for England. The white cliffs along the beach reminded him, he said, of cliffs on the south coast of England. He had a statement about the claim inscribed on a square piece of brass, which was then nailed to a post on the beach. Soon afterward, with the treasure on board once more, Drake said good-bye to the Indians. He sailed across the Pacific and, after about a year, arrived home in England.

Four hundred years later, in January 1981, a man went walking on a beach near Santa Barbara, California, just after a heavy storm. He stumbled upon something strange, never seen before on that beach. Five large, long objects lay in a straight line in the sand and surf. Formerly buried completely in the sand, they were now exposed for the first time because the storm had washed away so much of the beach. The man reported his find promptly to the University of California at Santa Barbara. Soon the five objects were being examined in the university laboratories.

Because a hard layer of rocks, minerals, and tar up to six inches thick covered them, at first it was not clear what they were. Some people thought they were pieces of large pipe from oil wells that had been in the area years before. The rock was then partly chipped away from one of the objects. This revealed something far more interesting than oil pipes. The discoveries were cannons—old iron cannons!

Two of them were taken to a U.S. Naval Station to be x-rayed. The Xrays gave a better idea of what they looked like underneath the rock and tar. They resembled cannons made in the sixteenth or seventeenth century—the sort that Francis Drake might have used.

Could they have been some of the cannons that Drake carried on *The Golden Hind*? A writer named James Gilmore, living in Santa Barbara, became interested in this idea. He met archeologist Jack Hunter, who specialized in studying things found in water. They examined both the cannons and

The cannons as they appeared when first found on the Goleta beach near Santa Barbara in January 1981. (Office of Public Information, University of California at Santa Barbara)

the histories of Drake's visit to the California coast. When, however, they announced their conclusion that these cannons were indeed from Drake's ship, an argument sprang up.

The reason for the controversy is this. For many years, people have believed that it was San Francisco where Drake came ashore, far up the coast from Santa Barbara. The main evidence is the account supposedly written by the chaplain on *The Golden Hind*. It states that Drake sailed north as far as where Seattle, Washington, is today. Then he turned back and found the calm bay at a certain distance from the point where he changed his course. This would have been around San Francisco Bay, where there are good harbors. A beach near San Francisco does, in fact, have white cliffs.

Another piece of evidence turned up in 1936. A square brass plate was found on a rocky hillside near San Francisco. It bore this message:

BEE IT KNOWNE VNTO ALL MEN BY THESE PRESENTS
IUNE. 17. 1579
BY THE GRACE OF GOD AND IN THE NAME OF HERR
MAIESTY QVEEN ELIZABETH OF ENGLAND AND HERR
SVCCESSORS FOREVER I TAKE POSSESSION OF THIS
KINGDOME WHOSE KING AND PEOPLE FREELY RESIGNE
THEIR RIGHT AND TITLE IN THE WHOLE LAND VNTO HERR
MAIESTIES KEEPEING. NOW NAMED BY ME AN TO BEE
KNOWNE VNTO ALL MEN AS NOVA ALBION.
C FRANCIS DRAKE

The plate fit the description in the chaplain's report. It looked like a piece of brass that could have been taken from a sixteenth-century ship. Examination of the metal by microscope suggested that it was old. At the time this discovery seemed to prove that Drake had been at a spot near San Francisco Bay.

Since the discovery of the cannons, however, Gilmore and others disagree with these claims. First, they argue, the report

The plate of brass supposedly left in California by Drake, and discovered near San Francisco in 1936. (The Bancroft Library, University of California at Berkeley)

about where Drake found the calm bay could have been wrong. It would have been a rather large error—since Santa Barbara is about 450 miles by sea south of San Francisco—but not impossible. In those days, knowledge about sailing in unknown waters was still limited and instruments for navigation were not very good. Also, Drake apparently was not a skillful navigator. He could have made a mistake, or the information could have been reported incorrectly.

Certain characteristics of the beach at Santa Barbara suggest that it was a likely place for Drake's landing. The spot where the cannons were found, called Goleta Slough, is now beach, but in the past it was a good harbor. Natural tar is

Archeologists and students carrying one of the cannons from the beach. (Office of Public Information, University of California at Santa Barbara)

found in the ground, which would have been useful in repairing *The Golden Hind.* As for the cliffs that reminded Drake of England, the Santa Barbara beach also has white cliffs.

But why would Drake have left the cannons behind? Very possibly, Gilmore says, just to make the ship lighter. Ahead of him lay a sail across the Pacific, and the *Hind* was overladen with treasure. The five iron cannons were far less valuable than the others, which were all of brass. Later, in fact, when the ship got stuck on a reef, Drake had his men throw overboard eight cannons—plus three tons of cloves. He was more willing to lose his armaments and other valuable cargo, it seems, than his booty in gold and silver.

Have other artifacts from *The Golden Hind* been found near Santa Barbara? Possibly. A heavy ship's anchor, eight feet long and of an old design, was discovered near the same spot in 1891. Used for years as a hitching post, it was rediscovered in 1965. At that time an anchor expert studied it and said it was exactly the type that would have been used on Drake's ship. The anchor could have been left behind, on purpose or by accident, after the *Hind* was tipped over on its side for repairing.

What about the brass plate found near San Francisco? Though it looks authentic in many ways, it is still a puzzle. Some scholars say the writing is not really like that of sixteenth-century England, and some of its spelling is too modern. The date on it is written in the American style—June 17, 1579—rather than the English way, 17 June 1579. In 1976, the metal was analyzed again at the University of California at Berkeley. This time more advanced techniques were used. Metal experts decided that the brass was not made in the sixteenth century. The plate now appears to be a forgery, but some people still believe the earlier tests were accurate and the plate is authentic.

The puzzle of the cannons would be solved, of course, if Francis Drake had reported that he left five big guns and an anchor on the beach in Nova Albion. That would be historical evidence. But the report he gave to Queen Elizabeth was apparently concealed and has not been seen since that time.

Therefore, the cannons have to be identified by a combination of archeological and historical methods. The artifacts themselves must be carefully studied and compared with information about the ways heavy guns were made in the past. This is a kind of *historical archeology*, which means the archeological study of artifacts and sites that date from historical times.

Just as artifacts in the ground have to be excavated with great care, the cannons first must be cleaned and preserved. This is no easy matter. The iron, long adapted to sea water and protected by the covering of rock and tar, can be damaged by exposure to air. Thus far, only two of the cannons have been cleaned.

The design of the cannons must then be studied. Before the 1700s, there were no standard models for cannons. Each country in Europe made its big guns differently. These cannons turned out to be definitely of English design.

The way the cannons were manufactured provides another clue in the mystery. One basic question concerns the metal used in them. The amount of carbon found in the iron suggests that it was cast in furnaces fired with charcoal. That would date the cannons before 1750. Another examination of the iron shows that separate parts of the cannons were probably made in different furnaces. The likely reason is that before the seventeenth century, furnaces were too small to handle large amounts of metal at one time. An expert on metals also studied the iron in the large anchor found at Goleta Slough. He said it appears to have come from the same source as the iron in the cannons.

Other facts about the cannons are also important pieces of the puzzle. The two cannons that have been cleaned are approximately five feet long, about three feet shorter than most cannons made in the late sixteenth and seventeenth centuries. They weigh only 608 and 643 pounds. This means they are surprisingly light compared with the weight of ball they fired, which was probably four and one-half pounds. There are two possible explanations. One is the small sixteenth-century furnaces, which could not cast the longer and heavier cannons used later. The other is that these cannons may have been manufactured when gunpowder was relatively weak. When gunpowder was made more powerful, by methods adopted in the late sixteenth century, cannons then had to be cast of heavier metal.

Also, the hole through which the balls were shot, called the bore, was made slightly wider at the open end of the barrel. This was true of cannons that fired stone balls. Stone shot, considered superior to iron shot, was used until the end of the sixteenth century, when it became too expensive to manufacture. All these facts suggest that the cannons were made around the middle of the sixteenth century.

Another clue may be found in "trade marks." In the past, gunmakers usually put an initial on a certain part of the cannon. What appears to be an H has been found on two of the cannons. In sixteenth-century England there were several well-known gunmakers who could have used the initial H.

James Gilmore, who first promoted the idea that the cannons once stood on the decks of *The Golden Hind*, therefore sticks to his guns. But other people still believe the cannons belonged to other ships that came to grief near Santa Barbara in the sixteenth century—or in the seventeenth, or the eighteenth, or even the nineteenth century! The debate goes on.

Was it really Sir Francis Drake who left his cannons on the beach? Was the first New England, named forty-one years before the Pilgrims landed at Plymouth, really Santa Barbara? Or was it San Francisco, as has long been thought? These questions may be answered soon, or argued for years to come. The possibility that the cannons may change a historical "fact" accepted for four hundred years is still an archeological mystery.

11

Has Gloucester Point Vanished Forever?

A FEW years ago, a marine science institute in southeastern Virginia decided on some major construction projects. There was nothing unusual about this—except that the institute sits on top of one of the oldest towns in the country. That town was Gloucester Point, a place not many Americans now know about because it has been buried for so long. Nevertheless, Gloucester Point represents a thick slice of American history. Today, because of twentieth-century construction, the future of its last remains is uncertain.

The site of Gloucester Point is a small peninsula on the York River across from Yorktown. Its story goes back to 1608, when the peninsula was first named on a map. In 1633, a tobacco warehouse was built on the point, which had a small natural harbor for shipping. Settlers came soon afterward. Later in the seventeenth and eighteenth centuries, several wealthy merchants and plantation owners lived in the community. Gloucester Town, as it was then called, was nearly selected as the capital of the colony in 1677.

The town's location on the river gave it strategic importance, protecting the river traffic and the communities farther inland. Therefore, a series of forts was built at Gloucester Point. The first one, in 1667, was designed as defense against attacks by the Dutch and other foreign ships. The colony records show that it was supposed to have earthen walls ten feet high and ten feet thick.

Gloucester Point played important roles in two major wars. Near the end of the American Revolution, the British commander Lord Cornwallis took over the peninsula. He fortified it heavily as part of his last stronghold against the American and French forces. After their defeat in October 1781, the British surrendered with full ceremony at Gloucester Point as well as at Yorktown. During the Civil War, Gloucester Point was occupied by both North and South. First the Confederate Army constructed new fortifications on the point, with eighteen large cannons. Then, in 1862, the fort was taken by Union forces, who held it until the end of the war.

All this is known from historical records. But strangely, the old town of Gloucester Point seems to have disappeared from history after the Civil War. It had been lived in for nearly two hundred and fifty years as a commercial center, a town, and a military fort. Then it was gradually abandoned. Many of the town and county records, furthermore, were destroyed during the Civil War. Although eventually a modern community by the same name grew up several miles inland, there was little left to tell about historic Gloucester Point—except the buried ruins.

In 1931, the National Park Service recognized the site as historically important because of the Battle of Yorktown, which included Gloucester Point. It was not, however, until 1978, when the construction plans came up, that the historic site began to be noticed once more. By that time the property belonged to the Virginia Institute of Marine Science, part of the College of William and Mary nearby in Williamsburg.

The institute's plans for construction included an expansion of the septic system and, later, a new administration building. When, in 1980, the area intended for the first project was tested for archeological remains, important ruins were found under the soil. The Virginia Historic Landmarks Commission made arrangements to study them. Just as bulldozers were starting to move earth at the site, archeologists and a crew of volunteer helpers started their own work. They were trying to learn as much as possible about the site in the two or three months available to them. Often they worked alongside the bulldozers.

The excavation uncovered remains of the Civil War fortification, part of which still stood above ground. In the center of the fort was a well, in which a belt buckle and a canteen belonging to the Union Army were discovered. The excavators also came upon many earlier remains in the same area, such as brick foundations from the first Gloucester Town, root cellars, post holes from three centuries, and a colonial trash pit. Traces of seventeenth-century fortification came to light as well, a faint reminder of the fort built in 1667. Artifacts of good quality, such as pieces of porcelain and part of a fine brass holder for a candle snuffer, were found near remains of houses. This indicated that many of the colonial residents were prosperous.

Ground-breaking for the modern administration building was scheduled for the fall of 1982. Again the archeologists and volunteers got busy learning what they could from the site. In this area they found brick foundations of a seventeenth-century house. Later, when construction of the new building was actually under way, a large trash pit from colonial times was discovered. Knowing that the site was going to be destroyed the next morning, volunteers turned their car headlights on and dug all night, trying to find as many artifacts as possible. In that short time, they recovered about six hundred pounds of eighteenth-century pottery sherds and other items.

In the spring of 1983, the Institute of Marine Science went ahead with plans for a parking lot. When the digging started, several graves appeared—part of a military hospital graveyard from the time when the British occupied Gloucester Point. A few graves were already cut into by electrical lines. Eight of the burials were excavated, studied, and removed to a nearby churchyard. Many others, however, doubtless still lie under the parking lot and buildings.

A trench revealing brick foundations from an eighteenth-century building, cut through by nineteenth-century brick foundations. (Photographer, David Hazzard)

Archeologists and volunteers carefully excavating part of the Revolutionary War graveyard at Gloucester Point. (Photographer, Peter Nebergall)

One skeleton found in this Revolutionary War burial place was that of a young woman. Her chest bones were curiously flattened. Archeologists wondered whether she could have strapped her chest very tightly for a period of time—perhaps to disguise herself as a soldier. A second possibility is that, as a child, she had worn stays, a tight, stiff corset intended to make a person stand very straight. In that case, she would probably have been from a wealthy, upper-class family. But if so, why was she buried in an army hospital graveyard? Her story might be an interesting one indeed.

Another set of bones at Gloucester Point also hinted at a little incident. The skeleton of a young pig was found, its backbone twisted as though run over by a cart. Noting this, the archeologists also recalled one of the surviving historical records—a 1726 regulation stating that pigs would no longer be allowed to run in the streets. Could the death of the pig have helped bring about adoption of that rule? Or had someone run over the animal by accident and then tried to conceal the evidence?

At the end of the three hurried-up excavation projects, in spring 1983, the archeologists and volunteers had to stop digging and let the bulldozers take over. Other parts of Gloucester Point are still untouched. Undoubtedly much information about life in seventeenth-, eighteenth-, and nineteenth-century Virginia is still lying hidden.

For a while, it looked as though these last remains of Gloucester Point were in danger. The demands of the institute seemed to outweigh the archeological importance of the place. Now, however, the College of William and Mary, which owns the property, has officially recognized the archeological needs. When other construction projects are planned at the site, adequate archeological study will be undertaken first.

Furthermore, Gloucester Point's importance has been underlined by its addition, in June 1985, to the National

Revolutionary War burials; a parking lot curb half covers those on the right, and a trench for electrical wires cuts right through them. (Photographer, David Hazzard)

Archeological director David Hazzard watches as a bulldozer destroys the site where his team has been trying to save a fragment of this nation's historic heritage. (Photographer, Peter Nebergall)

Register of Historic Places. Now there is hope that this historic site will not vanish forever.

The work at Gloucester Point illustrates historical archeology. At this site, archeological discoveries confirmed or shed new light on what was already known from historical records. As a result, much more is now understood than would be possible from the historical reports alone.

There is, however, a deeper meaning to the story. What went on at Gloucester Point was a dramatic case of *salvage archeology.* This kind of archeological work, also called rescue archeology, is aimed at studying sites that are threatened with destruction. It has become increasingly important in recent years.

As people build—houses, roads, anything to serve their needs—they often demolish what others did before them. In the past, it was only when remarkable ruins were found that people stopped to think about the old. Otherwise, traces of former times, such as the Indian mounds, were simply destroyed.

Today, however, they are not destroyed quite so freely. Americans are increasingly aware of the importance of protecting our national heritage. Since 1969, laws have helped to prevent reminders of our country's past from being heedlessly wiped out. Where new construction projects on public land are started with U.S. Government money—such as factories, housing, dams, schools—the land must be studied first. The builders have to understand the effect their project may have on the environment. Sometimes traces of people who once lived or worked at that spot are found. These remains are examined, and if possible preserved, before the new construction can go on.

No longer, therefore, is archeology a matter only for scholars and others interested in the past. Archeology has also become a public concern, because it is helping to preserve this nation's heritage for everyone. However, as more and more new construction goes on, sites that may be archeologically valuable disappear faster and faster. That is why public awareness and support for salvage archeology are so important.

Many archeologists today are involved in salvage archeological projects. Each situation is a little different. If the site appears important enough, sometimes the construction plans may be changed and the traces of the past saved. Occasionally, where enough has been learned about the site, a reconstruction can be built in another place. The Woodhenge near Kansas City is an example. Most often, however, archeologists are only able to learn and save what they can from the site before having to give way to the new builders.

Salvage archeological work frequently has to be carried out in haste, so that the developers' plans will not be delayed too long. Archeological teams working under pressure often need all the help they can get. They welcome volunteers, from teenagers to retired persons. A good way to learn about nearby archeological projects that need help is to inquire at the Department of Anthropology or American Archeology at the nearest university or college. Local historical and archeological associations also have information.

Some puzzles about the past may be uncovered at a salvage archeology site, and perhaps even some answers. But whenever a site is destroyed before it can be thoroughly studied, one mystery always remains. The archeologists must face such questions as these: What more could have been learned? Was there valuable information in a part of the site that could not be excavated? Has the chance for better understanding of these people of the past, and the events that took place at this site, been lost forever?

These questions linger over Gloucester Point. Here, new buildings and parking lots now cover the very places where, for more than two hundred years, people carried on their daily business, struggled with conflicting loyalties, and lived full lives. Those lives witnessed the birth, early growth, and crucial turning points of our nation. The few traces left of them could still be meaningful for our own lives.

What lies ahead? Can Americans take steps in time to prevent the loss of other important parts of our national heritage?

Fortunately, among the many young people today who are helping with salvage archeological projects like that at Gloucester Point, there are some who will become the archeologists of tomorrow. They may possibly find some answers to puzzling questions about America's past, or even discover new mysteries. In any case, they will add to future Americans' understanding and appreciation of the long, long story of this country.

Appendices

Glossary

A.D.—abbreviation for *Anno Domini,* which means "in the year of our Lord"; refers to the years since the birth of Jesus Christ

Anasazi—the name given certain Indians who lived in parts of the Southwest during the period A.D. 500–1300; a Navajo word meaning "the ancient ones"

Archaic—a stage in prehistoric Indian culture before the appearance of agriculture and pottery, lasting from about 10,000 to 3000 B.P.

archeology—the study of people of the past based on whatever they left behind, except for written materials; also spelled archaeology

archeo-astronomy—the study of prehistoric peoples' ways of observing the movements of the sun, moon, and stars

artifact—any object made or used by human beings

B.C.—abbreviation for "Before Christ"; refers to the years before the birth of Jesus Christ

B.P.—abbreviation for "Before the Present"; used for long-ago dates, with the year 1950 as the point from which to count back

cairn—a pile of stones erected as a monument or landmark

context—the undisturbed place or situation in which an object is found in an archeological excavation; includes surrounding soil and nearby artifacts

culture—the way of life followed by a group of people; includes beliefs, speech, behavior, and artifacts

dating—various techniques for determining the approximate time in the past when a plant or animal was alive, when an artifact was made, or when a site was used

earthwork—any large construction made of earth, particularly geometric figures and animal effigies

effigy—an image that represents a person or animal

equinox—the two times of year when days and nights are of equal length, and the sun rises and sets directly east and west; occurs around March 21 and September 21

excavate—to dig an archeological site systematically

grave gift—object buried with a dead person; also called a grave offering

henge—a large circle constructed of earth, stone, or wood

history—the account or study of people on the basis of records written by or about them

historical archeology—the study, by archeological methods, of the remains left by people who lived in historical times, or at a time when written records about the people were made

Ice Age—the time when glaciers covered much of North America, lasting until approximately 10,000 B.P.

paleo—a prefix meaning ancient

petroglyph—a symbol or word carved on rock

projectile point—the chipped stone tip of a weapon such as a spear or arrow; often called simply a "point"

pueblo—a house of stone slabs and sun-dried mud, usually a large cluster of adjoining houses of this type

radiocarbon dating—a technique for dating long-dead plant or animal matter by measuring the amount of the radioactive isotope Carbon-14 remaining in the specimen; also called C-14 dating

salvage archeology—archeological excavation of a site that is about to be altered or destroyed by modern construction; also called rescue archeology

sherd—a broken piece of pottery or glass; also called potsherd or shard

site—a place studied by archeologists where people lived or carried on some activity in the past

solstice—the two times of year when the sun appears to change the direction of its travels. The summer solstice, around June 21, is the longest day of the year, and the winter solstice, around December 21, is the shortest.

tool kit—the collection of different types of stone and bone tools used by a group of early prehistoric people

trait—a distinctive characteristic of a culture, such as a particular type of object or way of doing something

tree-ring dating—a method of figuring out the age of wood by counting the number of growth rings and observing patterns in the ring formation

Archeological Sites Open to the Public

The following are places mentioned in the text. There are numerous other sites, many of which can be found in a list of National Parks.

Chapter 2	**Bering Land Bridge National Preserve,** Box 220, Nome, Alaska 99762 **Folsom State Monument and Museum,** Folsom, New Mexico 88419
Chapter 3	**Dighton Rock,** off State Road 24, south of Berkley, Massachusetts **L'Anse aux Meadows National Historic Park,** P.O. Box 70, St. Lunaire-Griquet, Newfoundland, Canada AOK 2X0 **Newport Tower,** Newport, Rhode Island 02840
Chapter 4	**Angel Mounds State Memorial,** 8215 Pollack Ave., Evansville, Indiana 47715 **Devils Lake State Park** (effigy mounds), U.S. Route 12, near Baraboo, Wisconsin 53913 **Effigy Mounds National Monument,** McGregor, Iowa 52157

Etowah Indian Mounds, Route 2, Cartersville, Georgia 30120

Grand Village of the Natchez Indians, 400 Jefferson Davis Blvd., Natchez, Mississippi 39120

Grave Creek Mound, Moundsville, West Virginia 26041

Ocmulgee National Monument, 1207 Emery Highway, Macon, Georgia 31201

Serpent Mound, State Road 73 (between Belfast and Locust Grove), Peebles, Ohio 45660

Spiro Mounds Archeological State Park, Route 2, Spiro, Oklahoma 74959

Wyalusing State Park (effigy mounds), U.S. Route 18, near Prairie du Chien, Wisconsin 53821

Chapter 5

Fort Ancient, Exit 29 off Interstate 71, near Lebanon, Ohio (mailing address: 6123 State Road 350, Oregonia, Ohio 45054

Fort Hill, State Road 41 between Sinking Spring and Cynthiana, in Ohio (mailing address: 13614 Fort Hill Road, Hillsboro, Ohio 45133)

Mound City Group National Monument, 16062 State Route 104, Chillicothe, Ohio 45601

Moundbuilders State Memorial, 99 Cooper Ave., Newark, Ohio 43055

Mounds State Park, 4306 Mounds Road, Anderson, Indiana 46013

Chapter 6

Mesa Verde National Park, Colorado 81330 (near Cortez, Colorado)

Chapter 7 — **Cahokia Mounds Historic Site,** 7850 Collinsville Road, East St. Louis, Illinois 62201

Chapter 8 — **Bighorn Medicine Wheel,** Bighorn National Forest, U.S. Route 14 A, 35 miles east of Lovell, Wyoming (for further information write to Medicine Wheel Ranger District, Box 367, Lovell, Wyoming 82431)

Chaco Culture National Historical Park, Star Route 4, Box 6500, Bloomfield, New Mexico 87413 (Although the sun spirals on Fajada Butte cannot be visited, other sites in Chaco Canyon are open to the public.)

Kansas City Woodhenge, Little Platte County Park, Smithville Lake, U.S. 169, Smithville, Missouri 64089

Chapter 9 — **"America's Stonehenge"** (Mystery Hill), near Interstate 93, North Salem, New Hampshire 03073

Chapter 10 — The cannons are not presently available to the public. The beach where they were found is Goleta Slough, Santa Barbara Beach, Santa Barbara, California.

Chapter 11 — **Gloucester Point,** Virginia 23062 (Well-preserved Civil War fortifications can be seen.)

Index